CORK TRAVE

2024

*The Ultimate Travel Guide to Ireland CORK, Top
Things to Do, Best Places to Visit, Hidden Gems,
Travel Budget, Tips and Tricks*

NOMAD NICK

Contents

Welcome to CORK!

On the southern coast of Ireland, Cork is a vibrant city. Formerly a maritime powerhouse, Cork is today a diverse university city with cheap cuisine and vibrant nightlife.

The second-largest city in Ireland and one of the most populated cities in the nation, Cork, is beautiful all year round. Many tourists flock to Mizen Head to take in the picture-perfect coastline beauty, climb over Gougane Barra, and kiss the Blarney Stone for good luck.

The city has several attractions, including historical castles, museums, art galleries, water sports, thrilling festivals, and day trips to picturesque towns and natural beauty.

In conclusion, Cork is a must-see while traveling to Ireland since it offers something for everyone. With the help of this Cork travel guide by *NOMAD NICK*, you can organize your trip, cut costs, and make the most of your time there!

14 GORGEOUS REASONS TO VISIT CORK IN 2024

Discover Cork's Rebellious Past

Visit places like the city's Military Museum at Collins Barracks, the Cork City Gaol, where revolutionary nationalist Constance Markievicz and other rebels were once imprisoned, or the prison at Spike Island, also known as "Ireland's Alcatraz" to learn more about the significant role Cork, known as "the rebel city," played in the Irish War of Independence.

Explore Cork's Ancient City Walls at Bishop Lucey Park

Although only minor portions of the ancient walls are now intact, Cork was originally a completely walled city with fortified gates at what is now known as the North and South Gate Bridges. It is thought that after sustaining significant damage during the 1690 Siege of Cork, the original walls and defensive towers were destroyed or left to deteriorate.

A piece of the city wall dating from the 17th century was uncovered in the 1980s when building Bishop Lucey Park, which is located at the historic medieval center of the city, together with artifacts from the era that are currently on show at Cork Public Museum.

Admire Architectural Grandeur: A Visit to a National Treasure

The Lewis Glucksman Gallery, created by Irish architects O'Donnell and Tuomey, has garnered several honors, including the Royal Institute of the Architects of Ireland's 2005 award for Best Public Building in Ireland.

The gallery's architecture, a museum of art regarded as the "cultural and artistic center" of the University College Cork campus, has also won awards from the UK Civic Trust and the RIBA.

Immerse Yourself in the Unique Corkonian Accent

One of Ireland's most distinctive accents, a melodic kind of Hiberno-English that is sometimes characterized as musical, is claimed to be spoken by people from Cork. For example, listen to an interview with Olympic medal-winning rowers Paul and Gary O'Donovan (from Skibbereen). The Cork accent has been mocked by comedians like Tommy Tiernan, although at least one study placed it among the top Irish accents.

Savor Cork's Vibrant Coffee Culture

Cork's first passion may be cuisine, but coffee is quickly overtaking it as a close second. The region is home to some of Ireland's top local coffee roasters, and Cork City is teeming with amazing cafés where you may sample their wares. Even an annual exhibition of the region's top independent coffee shops is held in January during Cork Coffee Weekend. If hot chocolate is more your style, a local favorite called O'Conaill's hot chocolate and coffee establishment is said to provide the best in the nation.

Enjoy the Delights of Ireland's Food Capital's Cuisine

Cork is deserving of its status as Ireland's culinary capital, due to the ideal synthesis of a wealth of top-notch regional suppliers and a plethora of talented and enthusiastic chefs. A love of fine food is obvious pretty much wherever you walk in Cork, whether you're perusing the overflowing booths at the centuries-old English Market or tasting cuisine at the greatest of the city's numerous cafés and restaurants.

Ring the Historic Shandon Bells

Since 1722, when it replaced another church that had been destroyed during the Siege of Cork, St. Anne's Church has stood on its present location in Cork's Shandon neighborhood. It has become a well-known landmark and is the city's oldest church still in service.

Because each clock in its clock tower displays a slightly different time, it is fondly known in the area as "The Four-Faced Liar." However, St. Anne's is most known for its bells, which were the source of the hit song "The Bells of Shandon." Visitors to the church may ascend 132 steps to the belfry where they can ring the six-ton set of eight bells—among the only original church bells from the 18th century still in use in the nation—and enjoy panoramic views of the city.

Step into History: Michael Collins' Last Night

Consider staying at Cork's Imperial Hotel on South Mall if you're interested in Irish history. Michael Collins, a well-known Irish revolutionary leader, spent his final night there. On August 22, 1922, Collins left from here on a tour of West Cork, but he was assassinated in the village of Béal na Bláth by Irish Republicans who were hostile to the Anglo-Irish Treaty he had assisted in negotiating.

Reach for the Stars at Blackrock Observatory

CIT Blackrock Castle Observatory, whose interactive Cosmos at the Castle display has been recognized globally as an exceptional themed attraction, moved into a 16th-century castle just outside of Cork City in 2007. Visitors get the opportunity to discover how the cosmos was created and get a better look at the night sky during the self-guided tour. The Observatory will start creating an outreach program in conjunction with the launch of Ireland's first satellite, it was recently revealed.

Awe-Inspiring Natural Beauty

An awe-inspiring natural scenery surrounds Cork. Discover the Old Head of Kinsale and Mizen Head's breathtaking cliffs and seaside splendor. Hike along the picturesque paths of Gougane Barra Forest Park or explore the enchanted forests of Fota Island Wildlife Park. Whether you're a lover of nature or just looking for peace and quiet, Cork's natural splendor is waiting for you.

Festivals and Events Galore

A city that knows how to have fun is Cork. It holds a variety of festivals and events all year long that appeal to a wide range of preferences. There's always something spectacular going on in Cork, from the Cork Jazz Festival and Cork International Film Festival to lively St. Patrick's Day celebrations and regional music and arts events.

A Gateway to the Wild Atlantic Way

The Wild Atlantic Way, one of Ireland's most legendary road journeys, can be reached perfectly from Cork. Visit stunning cliffs, secret coves, and attractive coastal communities as you travel through the wild west coast. Discover the charming areas that are close to Cork, such as Clonakilty, Bantry, and the Beara Peninsula.

Warm and Welcoming Locals

Cork residents are renowned for their friendliness and generosity. Interact with welcoming residents who are willing to share experiences, advice, and their passion for their community. You'll experience the real friendliness that distinguishes Cork's citizens whether you're conversing with a bartender, a merchant, or a bystander on the street.

CHAPTER ONE

History of CORK

Cork, which originates from approximately 600 AD and has survived to the current day, bears evidence of the many periods of Irish urban history. Its history began in the seventh century as a monastic community, when St. FinBarre is credited with building a monastery.

Legend has it that Cork's origins may be located in the calm Shehy Mountains, where the Lee River began. In the heart of these mountains lies a treasured pilgrimage site known as Gougane Barra.

The early monastery is claimed to have been constructed on an island in Gougane Lake by St. FinBarre, the patron saint of Cork. Later, after crossing across the river valley, he founded the monastery that would become St. Finbarre's Cathedral in Cork City. This prevalent myth of St. FinBarre continues to have a strong effect on the city's spiritual identity and origin story.

Cork's roots, according to folklore, may be located in the calm Shehy Mountains, where the Lee River began. In the heart of these mountains lies a famous pilgrimage site called Gougane Barra.

The early monastery was claimed to have been erected on an island in Gougane Lake by St. FinBarre, the patron saint of Cork. He later constructed the monastery that would ultimately become Cork City's St. Finbarre's Cathedral after journeying across the river valley. This ubiquitous myth of St. FinBarre continues to have a significant impact on the city's spiritual identity and foundation story.

Cork has seen tremendous suburbanization as its population has grown over the last century. Bishopstown, Wilton, and other areas are in the southern hills, whilst Knocknaheeny, Gurranabraher, Sunday's Well, and other areas are in the northern suburbs. Cork, on the other hand, has some unknown treasures tucked away in its corners.

Cork's identity is changing as citizens contribute their thoughts and carve out niches in the city's culture. The River Lee has been a constant in Cork's history, seeing its transformation from a monastic town to a worldwide twenty-first-century city.

The marshy islands that formed Cork's original topography are referred to by the Irish name "Corcaigh," which means "marshes." The city core is located at the lowest point of the Lee River's confluence with the sea. Cork's rich history and deeply established sense of self as a port town have been shaped by its maritime location.

Cork's genuine peculiarity, however, is found in its population rather than in its natural environs. Corkonians are noted for their brilliance, self-assurance, and rebellious nature. Their culture is preserved via songs and oral traditions. Everyone who visits can notice how welcoming the residents are since there are always lovely conversations waiting for you on the streets.

As you stroll along St. Patrick's Street, often known as "Pana," you can experience the kindness of the residents, as well as the distinctive accent, bright energy of a huge city, and strong sense of belonging. Cork is more than just a city; it has a heart that beats in time with the tenacity and kindness of its people.

The Butter Museum

Have you ever wondered how butter was manufactured hundreds of years ago? The solution may be found in the Butter Museum. Step inside this museum, which is set in a magnificent 19th-century market structure, and you'll be transported back in time. Learn about the historical ways of butter making by exploring the exhibitions. From ancient ways to recent inventions, delve into the colorful history of this gastronomic mainstay. Learn about the evolution of butter manufacturing, learn family secrets, and discover Ireland's rich butter legacy. The adventure, however, does not end there. You will get the rare opportunity to try your hand at churning butter yourself at the Butter Museum. This allows you to enjoy the thrill of making butter using the same ways as professionals.

Fitzgerald Park

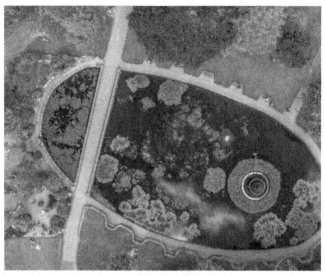

Take the family to Fitzgerald Park for a fun-filled and gorgeous adventure. With its spacious grounds ideal for leisurely walks and relaxation, Park has something for everyone. Take in the splendor of the park's rich foliage and colorful flowers, which create a tranquil mood. The amazing playground, where children may climb, swing, and slide to their hearts' content, will delight them. While wandering around the park, don't miss the historic sculptures and monuments that narrate the tale of corks. The finest part? A rich heritage. Admission is completely free, so you can have a terrific day out without breaking your wallet.

Saint Anne's Church

When seeing Cork, be sure to take a stop at Saint Anne's Church, commonly known as Shandon Church. This architectural gem in the vibrant Shandon area is a sensory delight. And it's full of fascinating stories. Saint Anne's Church, built between 1722 and 1726, is a remarkable testimony to Cork's rich legacy. Its magnificent Pepper Potts people and the harmonized sound of eight bells are breathtaking. Not to mention the charming fish weathervane sitting on top, which adds a bit of Ramsey to the cork skyline.

Visit this masterpiece to learn about its historical importance. Pay close attention to the lovely sound of the North Side bells, since the locals think that being born within earshot of them makes you a real Corkonian.

Spike Island

Are you looking for a more exciting adventure? Take a look at Spike Island. This beautiful site, located just off the shore of Cove in Cork Harbour, is a dream come true for history fans and adventure seekers.

This island has been used as a monastery for more than 1300 years. It's no surprise that Ireland's Alcatraz is commonly referred to as a fortress, jail, and even at home. Don't pass up the opportunity to take a guided tour once you get on the island. Is the finest way to properly appreciate the island's rich history and learn about the fascinating lives of its notable past inmates.

Elizabeth Ford

This amazing 17th-century star Fort welcomes you to explore its massive battlements and marvel at the awesome panoramic panoramas that open before your eyes as you dig into the city's colorful history and cultural past. While roaming over the fort's historic walls, you'll discover fascinating anecdotes that shed light on Cork's storied history. Elizabeth Ford serves as a living witness to the region's rich legacy, from the reverberating echoes of conflicts fought within its walls to the steadfast achievements of the city's tenacious spirit. Discover the interesting stories that pervade every stone as you explore farther, and take in the atmosphere of the carefully designed fortifications.

Blarney Castle and Gardens

Blarney Castle and Gardens is a medieval marvel that will take your breath away. Rich in centuries of enthralling stories and interesting legends. The castle, which was built in the 10th century, is a testimony to Ireland's rich legacy. Beyond the historic walls, though, there is much to uncover.

Prepare to be awestruck by the famed Blarney stone, which is claimed to grant the gift of eloquence when kissed. It's an opportunity you won't want to pass up. Don't forget to meander through the wide gardens that surround the castle while you tour it. These tranquil settings lend a magical touch to your vacation.

The English Market

The English Market, with its 218-year history, is an attractive gastronomic destination. This renowned attraction, located in the center of the city, is more than simply a food market; it's an engaging gastronomic excursion that highlights the finest of Irish cuisine traditions. Prepare to be captivated as you visit this colorful marketplace where local delicacies coexist with exotic imports from every vendor. However, this market gives more than simply a shopping experience; it also provides an opportunity to immerse oneself in an authentic Irish experience. Join the lively alleyways packed with energetic and cheerful chats.

BlackRock Castle

Observatory Stargaze at the BlackRock Castle Observatory and immerse yourself in the marvels of the cosmos. This old castle, which has been turned into a Science Centre, promises visitors of all ages an exceptional and instructive experience. This captivating location is wonderfully positioned along the tranquil. The River Lee's banks add to its enticing attractiveness. You'll go on a fascinating voyage through space as you explore the interactive displays and engaging exhibits, learning about the wonders of the universe, marveling at its heavenly bodies, and deepening your awareness of our role in the cosmos. The educated team is always available to answer your inquiries and concerns.

Cork City Gaol

Cork City Gaol is the place to go for a dose of history and culture. This amazing structure will transport you back in time to 1824 when it first received convicts through its formidable gates. People back then couldn't stop talking about it, dubbing it the best in the three kingdoms. Isn't that impressive?

Today, you may experience the allure of this architectural masterpiece firsthand by taking a guided tour or, if you prefer, one of their night excursions. The guides are knowledgeable and will bring the gaol's walls to life with exciting stories. Remember that you're following in the footsteps of some renowned inmates as you go through the hallways. Every turn reveals hidden truths and stories from the past.

Saint Patrick

St Stroll around Saint Patrick St., Cork's major retail street, to see what a typical Cork street looks like. It has an interesting combination of retail establishments and historic shops that sell corks. Cultural synthesis. Take your time and enjoy your stroll along this pedestrian walkway. a welcoming environment While taking in the colorful environment, you'll see local icons that lend appeal to the area, such as the exquisite facade of the Crawford Art Gallery or the famed Saint Patrick's Bridge. However, Saint Patrick Street is more than simply a commercial street; it also gives convenient access to entertainment venues and local attractions,

The Beara Peninsula

The lovely Beara Peninsula is perfectly situated between Bantry Bay and the Kenmare River. It is here that you will find a scenery that will stay with you forever. The Peninsula, undoubtedly one of the most gorgeous sites to visit in Cork, is best explored on foot, however, the Ring of Beara drive provides some of the best views.

Beara's two mountain ranges (the Caha Mountains and the Slieve Miskish Mountains) make it a beautiful site to trek, and the Beara Way route is worth committing to for a week. This peninsula is home to some of Cork's greatest wild camping spots as well as an abundance of charming tiny coastal communities.

Mizen Head

Many travel guides to Ireland list a visit to Mizen Head as one of the greatest things to do in Cork. The Mizen signal station was built to safeguard sailors traveling near Ireland's most south-westerly point. Visitors can first explore the Maritime Museum before making their way down to the signal station. On a windy day, strolling across the arched bridge above is an adventure in and of itself. Nearby Brow Head, which appeared in a Star Wars film, is also worth spinning up to.

Barleycove Beach

Some of the nicest spots to explore in Cork are the sandy stretches that are scattered throughout its lovely coastline. There is something to pique every interest, from popular tourist destinations like Inchydoney Beach and Garretstown Beach to lesser-known locales like Warren Beach.

Bantry House and Gardens

The Earls of Bantry's ancestral house, Bantry House and Gardens, is our next visit. It is beautifully positioned on a spot with a view of Bantry Bay.

In 1946, the mansion and its immaculate grounds were made available to the public.

Visitors can relax with a snack in the tearoom or go for a stroll on the grounds. Due to the lofty vantage point from which you can see the house and the harbor beyond, this is one of the most well-known Cork attractions.

Gougane Barra

There are few sites in the world, let alone Ireland, that can compare to the magnificent Gougane Barra. Visitors will find a huge valley and lake surrounded by mountains that climb up to 370 meters in height.

If you're wondering, "Is that yoke a small church?" it is! According to legend, in the sixth century, St. Finbarr (the Patron Saint of Cork) established a monastery on the little island of Gougane Barra Lake.

The current little church on the island is not the original, but it contributes to the fairytale-like setting at Gougane Barra.

The Ballycotton Cliff Walk

Few treks are as beautiful as the Ballycotton Cliff Walk. This is a fantastic ramble that will take you between 2 and 2.5 hours to complete, depending on your pace.

The views are spectacular throughout, and you'll get to see some beautiful hidden beaches, the Ballycotton Lighthouse, and much more.

Get yourself here if you're seeking spots to visit in Cork that will treat you to breathtaking vistas during your wander. You'll be chuckling as you finish with a bite to eat at Ballycotton Village.

Cobh

The buzzy tiny town of Cobh is home to many of the most popular things to do in East Cork, and it draws a large number of tourists.

When you arrive, park behind Cobh Cathedral (you won't be able to miss it). Explore this amazing piece of architecture before heading to the Deck of Cards viewing area (there are two).

At this moment, you'll be at the top of the slope. When you're ready, you may join the Titanic Experience tour, where you'll learn about the Titanic's first journey and her arrival in Queenstown (now known as Cobh).

You may then board the boat to Spike Island, often known as "Ireland's Hell." Over the span of 1,300 years, the island has housed a 24-acre fortification, a 6th-century monastery, and the world's largest prison depot.

The Baltimore Beacon walk

Many travel guides to Ireland include a visit to the Baltimore Beacon above as one of the greatest things to do in Cork.

It stands majestically at the entrance to Baltimore Harbor, where it has served as a warning system for seafarers for many years.

Following the 1798 Rebellion, the British ordered the building of the beacon. The existing edifice is thought to have been erected in the 1840s.

There's a little parking lot immediately next to the beacon that can accommodate 4 to 5 automobiles, depending on how people have parked. Park your car and walk up the steep hill adjacent to it. You won't be able to miss it.

Lough Hyne

This sea-water lake is set among undulating hills 5 kilometers from the vibrant small town of Skibbereen. It also serves as Ireland's first Marine Nature Reserve, complete with its ecology.

This Lough Hyne Walk leads you up Knockomagh Hill and provides breathtaking views of the lake and surrounding landscape.

It takes around an hour with pauses and is rather steep in sections. The ascent to the summit, on the other hand, is well worth the effort.

Healy Pass

The Healy Pass is one of the most unusual roads in Ireland. During the famine years of 1847, the pass was established to assist in preventing hunger.

It may be found in the Beara peninsula, where it leads vehicles, bikers, and pedestrians through the Caha Mountains on a unique and bendy path.

Such places make me joyful. They make you feel like you're on another planet.

Whale watching

Whale viewing in Cork is one of the county's most distinctive experiences but you are not guaranteed to see whales on any of the trips).

On one of these cruises, you could encounter anything from Basking Sharks and Harbour Porpoises to Sea Turtles and Jellyfish.

There's a 2-hour cruise that's "an exciting fun-packed coastal sightseeing tour of the West Cork coastline, featuring whale, dolphin, seal, and wildlife viewing," according to people who operate it.

Ireland's Teardrop And Cape Clear Island

Fastnet Lighthouse

Another fantastic trip that departs from Baltimore takes you to Cape Clear Island and then around Fastnet Rock on the way back.

You may take the boat to Cape Clear (45 minutes) and then take a shuttle bus to the island's historical center, where there is a multimedia display.

After you've finished with the exhibition, the final circuit of the tour takes you around Fastnet Lighthouse, also known as 'Ireland's Teardrop' (this is how it received its moniker).

The Donkey Sanctuary

Since its inception in 1987, the Donkey Sanctuary has cared for nearly 5,600 mistreated and abandoned donkeys.

Many of the donkeys who arrive at the sanctuary are receiving adequate treatment for the first time in their lives.

The group here cares for around 1,800 donkeys and mules (650+ of which live in individual guardian houses, while the remainder live on their four farms in the Liscarroll region).

You may visit the Knockardbane Farm and meet the farm's 130 donkeys and mules. If you're searching for activities to do in Cork with kids, this is the place to go!

Dursey Island

Ballaghboy, near the extreme extremity of the Beara Peninsula, is one of the most unusual things to do in Ireland. Of course, I'm referring to the cable car to Dursey Island.

Dursey Island Cable Car has been running since 1969. It spans an astounding 250m over the sea and takes only 10 minutes to cross.

On this delightful looping hike on Dursey, you'll be able to take in some unrivaled vistas of the Beara Peninsula.

The Youghal Clock Gate Tower

The Clock Gate Tower, located in the heart of Youghal, is perhaps one of the most popular things to do in East Cork town.

This historic monument, which stands 24 meters tall, has a colorful history spanning over 700 years, and you can learn everything about it on the tour.

The trip provides a one-of-a-kind sensory experience in the Merchants Quarters, where you can smell spices and sight silks. From the top of the tower, you can also see the jail cell and enjoy panoramic views.

Visit the Jameson Distillery

Plan a trip to the Jameson Distillery in Midelton if you're seeking for things to do in Cork with a group of pals.

Jameson lived in Dublin for about 200 years. Then, in 1975, they packed their belongings and relocated their flourishing enterprise to Midleton, Cork.

Whiskey enthusiasts may now join the highly recommended Jameson Experience Tour of the facility. This is a fully guided tour of the original Midleton Distillery that has received rave reviews online.

Clonakilty and its surrounds

Clonakilty has a lot to offer throughout the summer, and it's because of this that the town comes alive.

Begin your day with a stroll (or a paddle!) along the beautiful Inchydoney Beach.

Then, before entering the Michael Collins Heritage Centre, build up an appetite at the Clonakilty Black Pudding Visitor Centre.

To round off your day, head to DeBarras Folk Club and listen to live music while soothing your thirst with delicious Irish beers or Irish stout.

Charles Fort

Charles Fort, located near Kinsale, is a late 17th-century star-shaped fort associated with numerous key events in Irish history.

The most notable of these were the Williamite War (1689-91) and the Civil War (1922-23). You may take a self-guided tour of the fort, which will take you through the inside of the fort and through a variety of structures.

Doneraile House and Wildlife Park

Doneraile Court and Wildlife Park is another excellent option for families looking for things to do in Cork.

The estate spans the Awbeg River and is a delight to explore. There are various trails to choose from if you want to go for a walk.

You may also take the Doneraile Court Tour (ideal if it's raining) or go for a stroll in the beautifully groomed grounds.

Saint Finbarr's Cathedral

Saint Finbarr's Cathedral is a wonderful architectural gem that reflects the corps' cultural legacy well. It is an ideal location for architecture. Lovers, history buffs, and everyone looking for With its stunning Gothic Revival style, the cathedrals, three spires, and detailed facade will enchant you.

Stepping inside, you'll be greeted by the cathedral's grand interior, which emits a sense of calm and tranquility as you walk through it. Consider its historical significance for a minute. This holy location has the heritage of Saint Finbarr, who founded a monastery here in the 7th century, making it a place of great spiritual significance.

Ring the Shandon bells.

Don't pass up the opportunity to ring the Church of Saint Ann's famed shandon bells. These bells have come to represent the cultural and musical legacy of the city. Climbing the tower not only affords breathtaking views. Views of cork and its surrounds, but also an unforgettable experience.

As you grab the bell ropes, you'll feel a link to a centuries-long tradition and history. The church's architecture is stunning, with red sandstone and white ashlar limestone, and it leaves a lasting impact on visitors. Take time to absorb the beauty and immerse yourself in the colorful ambiance of this extraordinary location.

CHAPTER TWO

THINGS TO KNOW BEFORE YOU PLAN YOUR TRIP TO CORK

CORK Essentials

(Languages, Plug Types, Electricity, Currency, International dialing codes, Emergency Telephone number, Visa Requirements)

Languages:

Because English is the major language spoken in Cork, connecting with locals will be easy. However, you may occasionally hear the Irish language (Gaeilge) used in select regions, reflecting Ireland's rich linguistic legacy.

Plug Types:

Cork, like the rest of Ireland, utilizes Type G electrical outlets. The standard voltage is 230V, and the standard frequency is 50Hz. Bring the required adapters or converters to charge your electrical gadgets.

Electricity:

Cork's electrical supply is stable, and power interruptions are uncommon. During your stay, you may charge your gadgets with confidence and have continuous access to electrical services.

Currency:

Cork's currency is the Euro (€). ATMs are extensively available throughout the city, and credit cards are commonly accepted in most hotels, restaurants, and businesses.

However, it's a good idea to bring some cash with you for minor transactions and in case you wander into more isolated places.

International Dialing Codes:

To make an international call from Cork, dial 00 followed by the country code, area code (if applicable), and local number. If you need to contact Cork from another country, the country code for Ireland is +353.

Emergency Telephone Number:

In an emergency, dial 112 or 999 from any phone in Cork. These numbers will link you to the right emergency services, whether you require police, medical aid, or the fire department. Cork's emergency reaction is swift and effective.

Visa Requirements:

Before coming to Cork, be sure to verify the visa requirements for your nationality. For brief stays, many EU and EEA citizens do not need a visa. If you are from a non-EU/EEA country, you should check with the Irish embassy or consulate in your home country to understand the visa requirements and application procedure. Making sure you have the proper visa papers will allow you to have a stress-free stay in Cork.

Prices in CORK (Dishes And Drinks, Transportation, Accommodation, Best Hotels)

Cork, with its gorgeous scenery, historic charm, and active culture, is a city that draws visitors from all over the world. But, let's face it, we all want to keep a careful check on our wallets while visiting new places. So, here's your guide to making the most of Cork without breaking the bank.

Eating on a Budget:

- *Lunch and Drinks:* Local cafes and bars are great places to have a cheap lunch. A good pub meal will cost you between €10 and €15, and a pint of the famed Irish stout will cost you between €5 and €6. Some restaurants even offer meal packages that include a drink. Grab some fresh sandwiches or pastries from a local bakery and enjoy a picnic in one of Cork's gorgeous parks to save even more money.

Getting Around:

- *Transportation:* Cork is a small city that is simple to explore on foot. Many of the prominent attractions, such as the English Market and St. Fin Barre's Cathedral, are within walking distance. Public buses are relatively inexpensive, with a single travel costing between €2 and €3. If you plan to take public transit regularly, consider purchasing a Leap Card for lower rates which we explain more about in the next chapter of this guide.

Affordable Accommodation:

- *Best Hotels:* Cork has a variety of lodging alternatives to suit all budgets. Check out comfortable guesthouses or budget-friendly hotels like the Maldron Hotel Shandon Cork City and the Travelodge Cork for a budget-friendly stay. Prices for these choices normally range from €70 to €100 per night. If you're looking for more unique experiences, look into local B&Bs and hostels for even lower prices.

Dining Out:

- *Dinner:* Dining out in Cork does not have to be pricey. Explore the city's rich food scene by visiting ethnic restaurants and neighborhood cafés. A three-course lunch for one at a mid-range restaurant may cost between €25 and €35, excluding beverages. For a more affordable experience, look for street food sellers and takeout alternatives, where you can have a tasty dinner for roughly €10-€15.

Enjoying the Local Flavors:

- *Drinks:* When it comes to drinking in Cork, visit the city's lovely pubs. In a pub, a pint of Guinness or a local craft beer will cost you between €5 and €6. Happy hours and early evening offers may be a terrific way for budget-conscious tourists to enjoy Cork's nightlife without breaking the bank.

Festivals in CORK By Months

West Cork Rally - March

The West Cork Rally is a test of excellent rallying talents, with drivers traveling long distances to compete. Come and experience a terrific two days of excitement as you watch the many excellent drivers take on some great roads in West Cork.

Cork Choral Festival - April/May

Every year at the beginning of May, the Cork International Choral Festival in Ireland celebrates the absolute best of choral and vocal music. Prestigious international and national contests, gala and fringe concerts, public performances, and an education program are all part of the program. Follow the festival as it moves from one site to the next, including the Lewis Glucksman Gallery, the Honan Chapel on the UCC campus, St. Finbarr's Cathedral, St Francis Church, and many more.

Ballydehob Jazz Festival - April/May

Ballydehob Jazz Festival held at the end of April and beginning of May, features fantastic music in the pubs and streets, as well as street entertainment and a dealers fair where the masses enjoy good cuisine and beautiful craftwork while listening to the music. Some of the headliners included Michael Buckley, widely regarded as Ireland's best saxophonist today. Andreas Varady, a 12-

year-old Limerick guitar prodigy. The Samuel Hudson Quartet is headed by saxophonist Samuel Hudson, who lives in Berlin. The majority of the acts are free, so you may enjoy the Ballydehob Jazz Festival in a relaxing carnival atmosphere.

Bandon Music Festival - June

Bandon Music Festival is a music festival that started in 1996 under the name of a well-known jig, the first "Humours of Bandon" as a traditional music festival which then grew their wings to become the BANDON MUSIC FESTIVAL and some of the headline acts have included Hothouse Flowers and Juliet Turner, Mundy, Gerry Fish & The Mudbug Club, Aslan, the Saw Doctors, Mary Black, The Blizzards and Rethe public of Loose, Duke's Special, JackL, Delorentos and Fred. The music on the Music Trail was a combination of traditional sessions, folk, and rock. We are quite proud of what we consider to be one of Ireland's top music events.

West Cork Chamber Music Festival - June/July

The West Cork Chamber Music Festival features excellent music in locations such as St Brendan's Church, The Brick Oven Restaurant, Bantry, and Bantry House. Music by Schumann, Mozart, Fleishmann, Vivaldi, and others is available for guests to enjoy.

Cork Live at the Marquee - July

Aiken Promotions' Cork Live at the Marquee has previously hosted Diana Ross, Lionel Richie, Gypsy Kings, Tracy Chapman, Shayne Ward, Westlife, The Prodigy, Bell X1, Josh Ritterer, Lady Gaga, Anastacia, and many more fantastic bands.

Skibbereen Cork Arts Festival - July

Skibbereen Arts Festival has a lot to offer visitors. It has a great lineup of activities with many world-class national and international acts coming to town. The 4th Cork X Southwest Music Festival, a gala performance honoring Canon James Goodman, a superb Sound & Vision program of cinema and theater, and the extremely unique Skibbereen Children's Festival are all highlights. Abbeystrewry Church, with permission from Reverend Bruce Hayes, is an excellent setting for many of the activities.

Cobh Peoples Regatta - August

Cobh Peoples Regatta, a three-day August celebration with live music in pubs and the open air. Cobh Regatta is a wonderful day out for the whole family, including sailing competitions, a busking competition, the selection of the Cobh Peoples Regatta Queens, a fancy dress parade, bouncy castles, clowns, face painting, and much more.

Cork Folk Festival - September/October

Cork Folk Festival is one of Ireland's oldest traditional folk music festivals, held in September. Its survival is a monument to the passion and labor of its employees since it is put together year after year completely voluntarily by a committed group of enthusiasts, sometimes with the aid of large funding, frequently by a mix of numerous sponsors and supporters. Enjoy the essence of the indigenous music, song, and dance scene, where you may hear music from top national and international folk and traditional music practitioners.

Cork Jazz Festival - October

Cork Jazz Festival has been celebrated in October for nearly 40 years, and it lights up Cork with the sounds of jazz ringing throughout Cork City Centre. Follow the Jazz Trail to the numerous venues in and around Cork City, including The Gresham Metropole Hotel, The Imperial Hotel, Moran's Silver Springs Hotel, and many others. Cork Jazz is a fantastic weekend with some notable names from the jazz world.

Kinsale Fringe Jazz Festival - October

If you chance to be in Kinsale, the Kinsale Fringe Jazz Festival provides an alternate setting for jazz. In Kinsale, you may eat delicious meals while listening to easy listening or heart-pounding jazz.

Kinsale Gourmet Festival - October

The Mad Hatters Taste of Kinsale, an escorted tour of the 12 Members of Kinsale's Good Food Circle who will present spectacular dishes from their kitchens bearing testimony to the culinary skills of Kinsale's chefs, to a superb afternoon of fun and frolics with MC Derek Davis in the Fruits de Mer, Actons Hotel, Kinsale Suite.

Cork Film Festival - November

Corona Cork Film Festival is a renowned cultural event in Ireland. Since its inception in 1956, the festival has grown in size, number of admissions and attendees, notoriety, and media attention. The festival has grown in popularity among the general public, film enthusiasts, and filmmakers. Corona Cork Film Festival is well-regarded on a local, national, and worldwide scale. It is one of the most major social and cultural events in Cork city and region. The program is diverse, featuring a diverse mix of big-budget films, international cinema, creative indie films, documentaries, and short films from across the world. The festival is an important platform for Irish filmmaking.

Carrigaline Wren Boys Street Carnival - December

Carrigaline Wren Boys Street Festival, celebrated on St Stephen's Day, is a big street carnival that takes place on Main Street from 11 a.m. until 1 p.m. when traffic through the town is diverted. People dress up in bright costumes for the Wren Boy custom, and many people come to observe and participate in this yearly event. The South Union Hunt's yearly meet, with 15 pairs of hounds and over 100 horses, creates a stunning show as they march through the packed streets. On St. Stephen's Day, Carrigaline is the place to be.

Best Seasons to Visit CORK

Cork is situated in southwest Ireland. The North Atlantic Current keeps its temperature stable. The wettest seasons are late fall and winter.

While Cork's temperatures are approximately the same as Dublin's throughout the year, Cork experiences significantly more rainfall, particularly during the winter months.

Cork, Ireland - Best Times to Go

Cork is best visited between May and August. Early autumn is also ideal. The Guinness Jazz Festival takes place every October. The greatest months for bright and mild weather are July and August, but you'll have to share it with crowds of others.

When you go to Cork, you don't go for the weather. Be prepared for some rain, and have a good time. Cork's weather is pleasant and variable, even though it rains virtually all year.

Mornings and winters in the city are foggy. Despite this, Cork is one of the sunniest cities in Ireland.

Winter occurs in November, December, January, and February, with January being the coldest.

Spring: The months of March, April, and May are prime months for visiting Cork.

Summer is defined as June, July, August, and September.

The rainy season lasts from October through January.

CHAPTER THREE

ESSENTIAL THINGS TO KNOW AND PACK FOR CORK CITY

Packing Tips for Cork by Seasons and Months

When preparing for your vacation to Cork, Ireland, keep the ever-changing weather in mind. This gorgeous region of the world is famed for its lush green scenery and, you guessed it, regular rain. The Atlantic Ocean influences the Irish climate, so you may experience all four seasons in a single day. To ensure you're well-prepared for your journey in Cork, we've put together this thorough packing guide, which covers all you need to know about what to dress and what to carry each month.

January: Braving the Winter Chill

January in Cork may be extremely cold and damp. Temperatures are in the upper 30s°F (single digits°C), and rain is a common occurrence. Snowfall is regular, and cold may bite at your nostrils. Here's what to bring:

Clothes + Footwear:
- Fleece
- Jacket or coat
- Warm pants or jeans
- Lip balm

- Light gloves or mittens (extra for kids)
- Extra socks
- Sneakers or comfortable shoes
- A rain jacket to layer with your coat
- 100% waterproof footwear
- Rain pants
- Waterproof phone bag
- Umbrella
- Waterproof bag/luggage cover

Health:
- Hand sanitizer
- Travel disinfecting wipes
- Travel first aid kit
- Virus/bacteria filtering water bottle (due to potentially unsafe tap water in rural areas)
- Emergency motion sickness relief (pills or wristband)

Safety + Security:
- Anti-theft backpack
- Money/passport pouch
- Voice and data SIM card
- AirTag to track your luggage
- Comfort + Essentials
- Luggage scale to avoid fees
- Travel adapter (outlet type G)
- Power bank for devices

- Travel pillow
- Airplane phone mount

February: Cool and Rainy Days

Cork's weather is chilly and wet in February. Here's what to bring:

Clothes + Footwear:
- Extra socks
- Jacket or coat
- Warm pants or jeans
- Light gloves or mittens (extra for kids)
- Fleece
- Lip balm
- Sneakers or comfortable shoes
- A rain jacket to layer with your coat
- 100% waterproof footwear
- Rain pants
- Waterproof phone bag
- Wind-resistant umbrella
- Waterproof bag/luggage cover

Health:
- Travel first aid kit
- Hand sanitizer
- Emergency motion sickness relief (pills or wristband)
- Virus/bacteria filtering water bottle

- Travel disinfecting wipes

Safety + Security:
- Anti-theft backpack
- Voice and data SIM card
- AirTag to track your luggage
- Power bank for devices
- Airplane phone mount
- Travel voltage adapter (outlet type G)
- Luggage scale to avoid fees

March: Early Signs of Spring

Cork begins to thaw from the winter in March, but rain continues to fall. Here's what to bring:

Clothes + Footwear:
- Light and heavy skirts (light and heavy)
- Long sleeve shirts or blouses
- Light jacket or fleece
- Sneakers or comfortable shoes
- Extra socks
- A rain jacket to layer with your coat
- 100% waterproof footwear
- Rain pants
- Waterproof phone bag
- Wind-resistant umbrella
- Waterproof bag/luggage cover

Health:
- Travel first aid kit
- Hand sanitizer
- Virus/bacteria filtering water bottle
- Travel disinfecting wipes
- Emergency motion sickness relief (pills or wristband)

Safety + Security:
- Anti-theft backpack
- Voice and data SIM card
- AirTag to track your luggage
- Power bank for devices
- Airplane phone mount
- Travel voltage adapter (outlet type G)
- Luggage scale to avoid fees

April: Spring Blooms

April provides more nice weather to Cork, but showers are still prevalent. Here's what to bring:

Clothes + Footwear:
- Dresses
- Pants or jeans
- Light and heavy skirts (light and heavy)
- Long sleeve shirts or blouses
- Light jacket or fleece
- Sneakers or comfortable shoes

- Extra socks
- A rain jacket to layer with your coat
- 100% waterproof footwear
- Rain pants
- Waterproof phone bag
- Umbrella
- Waterproof bag/luggage cover

Health:
- Travel first aid kit
- Hand sanitizer
- Virus/bacteria filtering water bottle
- Travel disinfecting wipes
- Emergency motion sickness relief (pills or wristband)

Safety + Security:
- Anti-theft backpack
- Voice and data SIM card
- AirTag to track your luggage
- Money/passport pouch
- Power bank for devices
- Airplane phone mount
- Travel voltage adapter (outlet type G)
- Luggage scale to avoid fees

May: Mild and Pleasant

Cork in May has warm temperatures and little rain. Here's what you should bring:

Clothes + Footwear:
- Dresses
- Pants or jeans
- Light and heavy skirts (light and heavy)
- Long sleeve shirts or blouses
- Light jacket or fleece
- Sneakers or comfortable shoes
- Extra socks
- A rain jacket to layer with your coat
- 100% waterproof footwear
- Rain pants
- Waterproof phone bag
- Umbrella
- Waterproof bag/luggage cover

Health:
- Travel first aid kit
- Hand sanitizer
- Virus/bacteria filtering water bottle
- Travel disinfecting wipes
- Emergency motion sickness relief (pills or wristband)

Safety + Security:
- Anti-theft backpack
- Voice and data SIM card
- AirTag to track your luggage
- Money/passport pouch
- Power bank for devices
- Airplane phone mount
- Travel voltage adapter (outlet type G)
- Luggage scale to avoid fees

June: Early Summer Bliss

Cork experiences early summer temperatures in June. Here's what to bring:

Clothes + Footwear:
- Light and heavy skirts (light and heavy)
- Extra socks
- Long sleeve shirts or blouses
- Dresses
- Pants or jeans
- Travel shoe storage (if you have multiple shoe options)
- Light jacket or fleece
- Sneakers or comfortable shoes
- A rain poncho to layer with your jacket
- 100% waterproof footwear
- Rain pants
- Waterproof phone bag

- Umbrella
- Waterproof bag/luggage cover

Health:
- Virus/bacteria filtering water bottle
- Travel disinfecting wipes
- Emergency motion sickness relief (pills or wristband)
- Travel first aid kit
- Hand sanitizer

Safety + Security:
- Anti-theft backpack
- Voice and data SIM card
- AirTag to track your luggage
- Money/passport pouch
- Power bank for devices
- Airplane phone mount
- Travel voltage adapter (outlet type G)
- Luggage scale to avoid fees

July: Summer Sunshine and Showers

July offers mild weather to Cork but sometimes rains. Here's what to bring:

Clothes + Footwear:
- Dresses
- Travel shoe storage (if you have multiple shoe options)
- Light and heavy skirts (light and heavy)
- Sneakers or comfortable shoes
- Light jacket or fleece
- Pants or jeans
- Long sleeve shirts or blouses
- Extra socks
- A raincoat to layer with your coat
- 100% waterproof footwear
- Rain pants
- Waterproof phone bag
- Umbrella
- Waterproof bag/luggage cover

Health:
- Travel first aid kit
- Emergency motion sickness relief (pills or wristband)
- Hand sanitizer
- Travel disinfecting wipes
- Virus/bacteria filtering water bottle

Safety + Security:
- Money/passport pouch
- Anti-theft backpack
- Voice and data SIM card

- AirTag to track your luggage
- Power bank for devices
- Airplane phone mount
- Plug adapter (outlet type G)
- Luggage scale to avoid fees

August: Warm and Showery

August in Cork brings mild weather with a chance of rain. Here's what to bring:

Clothes + Footwear:
- Dresses
- Light jacket or fleece
- Sneakers or comfortable shoes
- Extra socks
- Pants or jeans
- Light and heavy skirts (light and heavy)
- Travel shoe storage (if you have multiple shoe options)
- Long sleeve shirts or blouses
- A rain jacket to layer with your coat
- 100% waterproof footwear
- Rain pants
- Waterproof phone bag
- Wind-resistant umbrella
- Waterproof bag/luggage cover

Health:
- Travel first aid kit
- Hand sanitizer
- Virus/bacteria filtering water bottle
- Travel disinfecting wipes
- Emergency motion sickness relief (pills or wristband)

Safety + Security:
- Anti-theft backpack
- Voice and data SIM card
- AirTag to track your luggage
- Money/passport pouch
- Power bank for devices
- Airplane phone mount
- Travel voltage adapter (outlet type G)
- Luggage scale to avoid fees

September: Early Autumn Strolls

In Cork, September symbolizes the beginning of fall. Expect cold temperatures and perhaps rain. What to bring:

Clothes + Footwear:
- Travel shoe storage (if you have multiple shoe options)
- Dresses
- Light jacket or fleece
- Long sleeve shirts or blouses

- Extra socks
- Pants or jeans
- Sneakers or comfortable shoes
- Light and heavy skirts (light and heavy)
- A rain poncho to layer with your coat
- 100% waterproof footwear
- Rain pants
- Waterproof phone bag
- Umbrella
- Waterproof bag/luggage cover

Health:
- Travel disinfecting wipes
- Travel first aid kit
- Virus/bacteria filtering water bottle
- Emergency motion sickness relief (pills or wristband)
- Hand sanitizer

Safety + Security:
- Money/passport pouch
- Anti-theft backpack
- AirTag to track your luggage
- Voice and data SIM card
- Power bank for devices
- Airplane phone mount
- Plug adapter (outlet type G)
- Travel neck support pillow
- Luggage scale to avoid fees

October: Autumn Colors and Rainy Days

Cork has cool temperatures and heavy rain in October. Here's what to bring:

Clothes + Footwear:
- Light and heavy skirts (light and heavy)
- Travel shoe storage (if you have multiple shoe options)
- Long sleeve shirts or blouses
- Extra socks
- Light jacket or fleece
- Dresses
- Sneakers or comfortable shoes
- Pants or jeans
- A rain poncho to layer with your coat
- 100% waterproof footwear
- Rain pants
- Waterproof phone bag
- Windproof umbrella
- Waterproof bag/luggage cover

Health:
- Hand sanitizer
- Travel first aid kit
- Virus/bacteria filtering water bottle
- Travel disinfecting wipes
- Emergency motion sickness relief (pills or wristband)

Safety + Security:
- Anti-theft backpack
- AirTag to track your luggage
- Voice and data SIM card
- Money/passport pouch

November: Chilly Days and Rainy Nights

November brings chilly temperatures and a lot of rain. Prepare for colder weather. What to bring:

Clothes + Footwear:
- Dresses
- Travel shoe storage (if you have multiple shoe options)
- Extra socks
- Sneakers or comfortable shoes
- Pants or jeans
- Long sleeve shirts or blouses
- Light and heavy skirts (light and heavy)
- Light jacket or fleece
- A rain poncho to layer with your coat
- 100% waterproof footwear
- Rain pants
- Waterproof phone bag
- Umbrella
- Waterproof bag/luggage cover

Hhealth:

- Travel first aid kit
- Virus/bacteria filtering water bottle
- Travel disinfecting wipes
- Emergency motion sickness relief (pills or wristband)
- Hand sanitizer

Safety + Security:
- AirTag to track your luggage
- Money/passport pouch
- Anti-theft backpack
- Voice and data SIM card

December: Festive Season in Cork

Cork had a cold and wet December. Embrace the holiday mood by dressing appropriately. What to bring:

Clothes + Footwear:
- Extra socks
- Fleece
- Light gloves or mittens (extra in case they get lost)
- Lip balm
- Warm pants or jeans
- Jacket or coat
- Sneakers or comfortable shoes
- A rain jacket to layer with another jacket
- 100% waterproof footwear

- Rain pants
- Waterproof phone bag
- Windproof umbrella
- Waterproof bag/luggage cover

Health:
- Hand sanitizer
- Travel first aid kit
- Virus/bacteria filtering water bottle
- Travel disinfecting wipes
- Emergency motion sickness relief (pills or wristband)

Safety + Security:
- Anti-theft backpack
- AirTag to track your luggage
- Money/passport pouch
- Voice and data SIM card

Comfort + Essentials:
- Airplane phone mount
- Plug adapter (outlet type G)
- Travel neck support pillow
- Luggage scale to avoid fees
- Power bank for devices

E-T-I-A-S: A Brief Introduction

The European Travel Information and Authorization System, or E-T-I-A-S, is your ticket to trouble-free travel in Europe. This visa, designed to increase safety and convenience, is now required for passengers from English-speaking countries such as the United States, the United Kingdom, Australia, and Canada.

In Addition to Your Travel Arsenal

Before you continue, keep in mind that the E-T-I-A-S Visa is a complement to, not a replacement for, your standard travel paperwork. Your passport is still your most prized item. Check that it is valid for at least three months beyond your intended return date.

Three-Year Validity – with a Twist

After successfully applying for the E-T-I-A-S Visa, you'll have it for three years. However, here's the catch: if your passport expires before three years, your visa's validity is also reduced. If you need to renew your passport, do so before applying for a visa.

Exemptions and Special Considerations

This visa does not apply to our EU compatriots. EU residents and those with residence cards or residency paperwork from EU nations are not required to obtain an E-T-I-A-S Visa to enter Europe. But keep in mind that this visa will not allow you to work, stay more than 90 days, or study. These undertakings necessitate the acquisition of different visas.

No Guarantees at the Gate

While the E-T-I-A-S Visa expedites your travel, it does not ensure your admission into the EU. Customs officers will still examine your eligibility upon arrival. So, be on your best behavior!

The Price of Access

The cost of obtaining an E-T-I-A-S Visa is a moderate 7 euros - a tiny investment for a more pleasant European vacation.

Pro Tip: Passport Planning

Those whose passports are about to expire should renew them before applying for the E-T-I-A-S Visa. This way, you won't have to worry about your visa being invalid when your passport is renewed.

Stay Informed

The official EU website is your best bet for detailed information on the E-T-I-A-S Visa. Keep in mind that as the program progresses, more information may become available. Keep an eye out for any further developments.

So, starting in January 2024, make sure you have your E-T-I-A-S Visa if you're coming to Europe from one of the nations where it's necessary. The secret to worry-free discovery is in your hands.

Getting Around CORK (Insider Tips)

Cork is a lovely city to explore on foot, by bike, or by public transportation. Renting a car might be a terrific way to visit more of the surrounding places. There are several attractions in and around Cork.

On Foot

Cork is a tiny and easily walkable city. Visitors may enjoy one of four heritage-related walking pathways in the city center ('Cork Walks,' view the Ard street art on foot, or discover Cork by taking one of many other self-guided and guided walking excursions across the city and county. Consider one of the numerous wonderful walking tours and walks available around the county, with routes to suit all abilities, as a fantastic opportunity to interact with nature in our gorgeous countryside.

We urge that all visitors respect the environment and practice the Leave No Trace principles of responsible stewardship throughout their stay, with the goal of minimizing any negative environmental and social consequences from outdoor activities.

By Bike

Cycling is an excellent way to save money while staying active. It is both environmentally friendly and generally the quickest way to get about. TFI Bike Share lets you rent bikes to navigate about Cork City simply and swiftly. There are approximately 30 bike dock spots around the city, making this the best method to travel about and see everything.

Bikes are available from 6 a.m. to 12 a.m. Journeys of 30 minutes or less are free, while guests with a credit card can sign up for a 3-day ticket. The TFI Bikes App is ideal for city cycling trips on TFI Bikes, including information on station locations, bike and stand availability, and route planning.

You may explore recommended routes on the Cork City Cycle Map. Alternatively, take a guided bicycle tour of the city or county, or participate in the Cork Cycling Festival.

By Bus

Buses are an excellent kind of transportation, particularly for longer distances.

Bus Éireann operates several services from Cork city center to all areas of the county, including towns and villages along the Wild Atlantic Way and Ireland's Ancient East. Cork's main bus terminal is located in the city center at Parnell Place; all intercity routes to the county depart from here. West Cork Connect also provides bus service between West Cork and the city center. Cobh Connect buses run between Cobh and Cork City, while the Local Link minibus network covers the entire county.

TFI Leap Cards, which are up to 30% cheaper than cash single tickets and may be used on Cork City bus services (run by Bus Éireann) as well as Cork commuter train services on the Cork-Cobh and Cork-Midleton lines, can be purchased.TFI Leap Cards, which are up to 30% cheaper than cash single tickets and may be used on Cork City bus services (run by Bus Éireann) as well as Cork commuter train services on the Cork-Cobh and Cork-Midleton lines, can be purchased.

By Train

Traveling by train allows you to put your feet up and gaze out the window at Cork's lovely green countryside. Cork's east rail network connects Cobh, the Titanic's final port of call, to Midleton (home of the famous Jameson Distillery). It goes from Cork City to Mallow in the west (Mallow Castle).

As previously stated, you may purchase a TFI Leap Card, which is up to 30% less expensive than cash single tickets and can be used on Cork City bus services (run by Bus Éireann) as well as Cork commuter train services on the Cork-Cobh and Cork-Midleton lines.

By Car

Although we urge tourists to take public transportation wherever feasible, if you want to travel off the beaten path and see some of Cork's hidden jewels in more rural regions, you may need to rent a vehicle or ride a motorcycle.

Cork is home to the majority of international automobile rental firms. A valid driver's license and a credit card are required to hire a car in Ireland. When renting a car, we advise tourists to regard the environment and opt for smaller, electric versions where possible.

- Remember that in Ireland, we drive on the left!

- Please be aware of the alcohol-related driving rules in Ireland. It is strongly advised that you never drink and drive for a safe and happy holiday experience.

Public Transportation in CORK

Visitors visiting Cork will discover an extensive bus network run by Bus Éireann. The majority of city bus routes run across the city and radially from the city center, making it simple to travel about. The buses may also take you to major tourist attractions like Blarney Castle.

A ticket in the center region starts at around €2.30. Higher fees apply if you travel further from the city center. Tickets for public transportation are often bought in cash.

If you want to use public transit frequently and will be in Cork for more than a few days, you might consider obtaining a Leap Card. The card lets you load money for travel and can save you up to 30% on bus tickets.

Public Transportation to Get Around FROM Cork

Irish Rail services from Kent Station in Cork's city center for visitors seeking to tour other cities in Ireland. InterCity services to Dublin are available every hour, with trip times as short as 2.5 hours.

Furthermore, commuter train services link Kent Station with a few other stations, and connections may be established to conveniently travel to almost all of Ireland's larger cities. Tickets can be purchased in advance online.

Travelers may easily pick a train that matches their schedule and budget with so many alternatives available. Best of all, you may enjoy the breathtaking beauty of the Irish countryside from the luxury of your seat.

Driving in Cork

I would not advocate driving if you are simply visiting Cork. The city is simple to navigate in other ways (walking, taxis, etc.), so having a car would be more trouble than it's worth in terms of locating parking and paying parking costs.

However, if you want to take a road trip across Ireland or go on day excursions from Cork to discover the countryside, you'll need a car. You may either hire a car in Cork and begin your road trip after touring the city, or you can choose accommodation that includes parking and store your car and forget about it for a few days.

Visitors who want to drive in Cork should be aware that Ireland travels on the left side of the road and should be mindful of one-way streets and limited parking choices.

Ticketing and Transport Passes in CORK

TFI Leap Card

TFI's Leap Card is a handy method to pay for public transportation in Dublin and nearby counties including Cork, Galway, Limerick, Waterford, Sligo, Athlone, Kilkenny, and Wexford. It can also be used on a variety of commuter and rural bus routes within the TFI public transportation network.

It eliminates the need to carry change, and TFI Leap Card rates are up to 30% less expensive than cash single tickets. TFI Leap Card holders in Dublin may also make use of smart discount features like fare capping and the Leap 90 Discount.

Leap Top-Up App

Leap Top-Up is free software available from the Google Play and Apple App stores for NFC-enabled Android and iOS phones. Download and launch the app on your NFC-enabled smartphone, then hold your TFI Leap Card to the back of the device to quickly check your balance and the past 5 transactions, receive a pre-paid ticket, or top-up your TFI Leap Card.

Single ticket

Single tickets can also be purchased from the bus or railway driver. Single tickets cost more than using a Leap Card.

Day ticket

In Cork, a day ticket entitles you to unrestricted travel on Bus Éireann, Cork Citybus, and Irish Rail services. Adult day tickets are €15.50, students €12, and children €9.

Weekly ticket

In Cork, a weekly ticket entitles you to unrestricted travel on Bus Éireann, Cork Citybus, and Irish Rail services. Adult weekly tickets cost €62, students €49.50, and children €31.50.

Monthly ticket

In Cork, a monthly ticket entitles you to unlimited travel on Bus Éireann, Cork Citybus, and Irish Rail services. Adult monthly passes cost €185, students €154, and children €102.

Student Leap Card

The national student travel card is the Student Leap Card. It offers reductions on fares for Go-Ahead Ireland, Dublin Bus, Luas, Bus Éireann, DART, and Irish Rail (Iarnród Éireann) services, as well as several other privately owned local services in the Republic of Ireland.

TaxSaver

Taxsaver, which was introduced in 1999, gives large discounts to encourage individuals to take public transportation to and from work.

Employers need just register online, acquire login information, and begin purchasing monthly or annual tickets for their employees, which are then applied to Personalised Leap Cards.

The cost of the Taxsaver ticket is removed immediately from the employee's income, and depending on the ticket type and your tax band, you can save between 28.5 percent and 52 percent othe ff the ordinary fare price.

The Taxsaver system is now being redesigned to offer a single entry point for Taxsaver clients, making the service more accessible to companies and employees.

Mobile ticketing (m-Ticketing)

The recently launched m-Ticketing (or mobile ticketing) experiment, 'TFI Go,' is the first stage of the NGT Programme, which comprises many initiatives aimed at providing users with new payment ways for public transportation services.

TFI Go is designed to be a multi-supplier, multi-platform solution that allows customers to purchase and activate their tickets via a mobile app before boarding public transportation. If the trial is successful, this contemporary, flexible, and frictionless ticketing system will eventually be rolled out across all transport operators in both urban and rural Ireland, improving the travel experience and providing an extra means to pay for travel, particularly longer distance travel.

TFI Go was originally tested on longer-distance Bus Éireann trips. The experimental phase began in mid-2020 on the Dublin to Wicklow service, with other commuter routes to be added over time.

The demand for contactless account-based ticketing solutions is likely to grow significantly in the near future, and TFI Go is the first component of an integrated program that will give a more comprehensive and creative "mobile first" service.

Transportation Tips And Rules Travelers' Need To Know

Benefits Of Using A TFI Leap Card

- It spares you from carrying change.
- TFI Leap Card rates are up to 30% less expensive than cash single tickets.
- TFI Leap Card holders in the Dublin region may additionally take advantage of smart discount features like fare capping and the Leap 90 Discount.
- You may use the Leap Top-Up App to check your balance, examine your past 5 transactions, pick up a pre-paid ticket, or top up your card.
- If you are a student, you may receive a Student Leap Card, which grants you fare reductions.

- If you are an employer, you may set up a TaxSaver plan for your employees, which provides them with fare reductions.
- On your smartphone, you may buy and activate tickets using the TFI Go mobile ticketing app.

What to Know About Renting a Car in Ireland

The most crucial things to know about renting a car in Ireland (particularly for tourists from the United States) are that you must drive a manual transmission (stick shift) vehicle and that you must drive on the left side of the road.

A valid driver's license and a credit card are required to hire a car in Ireland. To be able to drive in Ireland, you will also need to acquire insurance.

Keep in mind that distance and speed restrictions in Ireland are measured in kilometers.

Is It Worth Renting a Car in Ireland?

You will want to hire a car in Ireland if you want to explore anything in nature, smaller and more rural towns, or anything off the main route!

I usually urge my friends and family to hire a car so they don't lose out on the beautiful landscape and excellent things to do in Ireland's smaller villages and between the major cities.

To hire a car in Ireland, I recommend Discover Cars. They evaluate costs from the top Irish car rental providers to get you the BEST offers and the LOWEST prices.

Discover Cars saves you money on vehicle rentals, is simple to use, and, most importantly, allows you to see everything Ireland has to offer for the most unforgettable vacation!

They also offer insurance coverage, which is required in Ireland for driving. Discover Cars' convenience of acquiring insurance when renting a car is something I like. After you've reserved your car, you may pick it up at Cork Airport or wherever is most convenient for you.

Is Cork Safe for Tourists?

Cork is a lovely city with lots for visitors of all ages and interests. The ancient streets are dotted with stores and restaurants, and the River Lee runs through town. Cork is also recognized for being a safe resort, with low crime rates and a laid-back environment.

As a result, visitors may explore Cork with confidence and without concern for their safety. Of course, measures should always be taken while visiting any new site, but visitors can be confident that Cork is a safe city to visit.

CHAPTER FOUR

ACCOMMODATION, STUNNING BEACHES, HOTELS BY BUDGET, AND ACTIVITIES

Best Beaches in CORK City

Cork has some of the most stunning beaches in Ireland, with long sandy strands backed by dunes and rock pools perfect for exploration. You have your pick of places to lie out in the sun all day, play in the sand and water with the family, try your hand at water activities, or walk along the beach.

Youghal, Front Strand Beach

Youghal Front Strand Beach is in the county of Cork. It offers excellent amenities and is popular among locals for strolling.

Youghal, Claycastle Beach

Claycastle Beach is near the historic walled town of Youghal in County Cork. It is an excellent location for strolling, swimming, and resting. It is quite popular with both inhabitants and visitors.

Garryvoe Beach

Garryvoe Beach is a pebble beach in County Cork's settlement of Garryvoe. It is a popular family beach with a playground nearby.

Garrylucas, White Strand

Garrylucas, White Strand is a sandy beach in County Cork near the Old Head of Kinsale. It contains dunes in areas, as well as a public parking lot and restrooms.

Garrettstown Beach

Garretstown Beach is a large sandy beach on
the coast of County Cork. It offers
breathtaking views of the Old Head of
Kinsale and is ideal for trekking, bathing,
and swimming.

Inchydoney East Beach

Inchydoney East Beach on the small island of Inchydoney in County Cork features a range of magnificent scenery, ranging from towering grassy sand dunes to coarse, rocky cliff walls.

Inchydoney West Beach

Discover picturesque Inchydoney West
Beach, just a 10-minute drive from the quaint
West Cork town of Clonakilty. Swim in the
sparkling blue ocean and walk along its
broad golden coastline.

Warren Beach

Warren Beach is a tiny, rural sandy beach in County Cork located at the mouth of the Rosscarbery River.

Tragumna

Tragumna Beach is a tiny, picturesque, protected sandy beach near Skibbereen, County Cork.

Barley Cove

Escape to the magnificent strands of Barley Cove in West Cork for a day of beach fun with the family.

Where to stay in CORK: Best Areas and Neighborhoods

Whether you're visiting Cork to sample the burgeoning gourmet scene or simply traveling through County Cork Ireland to kiss the Blarney Stone, it's worth staying a few days to fully explore all of the fantastic things to do in Cork.

From exceptional events like the yearly jazz festival to day-to-day activities, Ireland's second-largest city is a fantastic destination for visitors.

Cork is a must-see city in Ireland since it is the country's second-largest city, just behind Dublin, and has its own culture. When organizing your vacation, you may difficult to select where to stay in Cork, but happily, there are several wonderful suburbs – you truly can't go wrong.

Visiting Cork is one of the nicest things you can do in Ireland. Whether you visit during the country's most prestigious jazz festival or simply for a quick day trip to see Blarney Castle, Cork will be one of the most memorable portions of your journey to the Emerald Isle.

This Cork lodging directory will inform you about all the greatest Cork neighborhoods so that you can organize your vacation more efficiently! Cork is truly one of the nicest locations to visit in Ireland.

Blarney

Blarney is one of the few sites in Ireland that everyone has heard of because it is home to the Blarney Castle and Gardens!

If this is your primary purpose for visiting this part of Ireland, staying in Blarney is the best place to stay in Cork.

This Cork suburb is not as noisy and crowded as the city, making it a more serene and charming place to visit. Blarney is also much smaller than Cork and is full of idiosyncrasies and wonderful eateries.

There is good public transit in this region of the nation, so don't worry if you don't have a car during your stay. Simply take the regional bus to go from Cork City to Blarney in 45 minutes.

Blarney Castle Cork 1

Anyone visiting Cork for the sole purpose of seeing Blarney Castle and Gardens should stay here.
This destination can be explored for a whole day, so staying in town allows you to be among the first visitors and escape the hordes that arrive later in the day.

Top Highlights in Blarney

- As previously said, the historic Blarney Castle & Gardens is a must-see attraction in Blarney.
- The Blarney Woollen Mills store is an excellent place to learn about Ireland's history via weaving from the nineteenth century.
- Ballincollig Castle, which has its grounds named the Ballincollig Regional Park
- Muskerry Arms, which also serves as a bed and breakfast and a pub, is a terrific place to eat.

Where to Stay in Blarney

Muskerry Arms, located just a short walk from Blarney Castle and the bus stop to Cork City, is the most economical place to stay in Blarney. Rooms start at €95 ($112) and go up depending on the room type.

The Blarney Woollen Mills Hotel, a 10-minute walk from Blarney Castle and directly next to the famed Blarney Woollen Mills store, offers more luxurious accommodation in Blarney. Rooms here start at about €108 ($127).

The Blarney Castle Hotel is the best location to stay in Blarney and is quite popular with couples and families. This hotel, which dates back to 1837, is just two minutes from both Blarney Woollen Mills and Blarney Castle. Prices begin at €122 ($144).

Cork City Centre 2

Because it is in the heart of everything, the city center is by far the greatest place to stay in Cork. By lodging here, guests may avoid using public transit and stroll to all of the main attractions, including bars, monuments, restaurants, and more.

Going on day trips is one of the many benefits of staying in the city center. If you want to travel on a day excursion from Cork, you can almost roll out of bed and head to a local pickup location because they are usually located right in the city center.

Because of the prominent location, prices in this area tend to be a little higher. Unfortunately, unlike many other cities in Ireland, there are no hostels in Cork's city center.

If you don't mind crowds and loud noises, this is undoubtedly the best spot to stay. This neighborhood of Cork is mostly popular with younger, lone travelers as well as people who enjoy being in the center of cities when traveling.
If you're just in Cork for a weekend, you should absolutely stay in the city center.

Top Highlights in Cork City Centre

- The English Market, an 18th-century market filled with great food vendors, is one of Cork's top locations to dine.
- Any day of the week, head to Crane Lane Theatre to hear live music.
- Market Lane, a family-friendly mid-range restaurant with an outstanding dessert, is another must-visit.
- Visit Cork City Hall to learn more about the history of County Cork.
- Stroll down St. Patrick's Street to find any department store you can think of.

Where to Stay in Cork City Centre

The Jurys Inn Cork, which is popular with families, is the most economical option to stay in the city center. It is close to Cork City Hall and the English Market, and rents start at €88 ($103).

The Maldron Hotel South Mall Cork City, located between Kent Train Station and the English Market, is a wonderful choice for couples. Rates start at €144 ($169) per night and vary based on the time of year you visit.

If you're seeking a 4-star hotel right in the heart of Cork's city center, the Imperial Hotel Cork City is the place to stay. With prices starting at €151 ($178), this is one of the best places to stay in Cork.

Victorian Quarter 3

If you enjoy history, the Victorian Quarter is the place to stay in Cork City. This is a lovely and modest Cork neighborhood famed for its 19th-century architecture and stunning structures.

The Victorian Quarter is home to hip restaurants, pubs, bars, bookstores, monuments, and museums, among other things. This is one of the more trendy locations to stay in Cork, and it's only a short walk from the city center!

However, unlike in the city center of Cork, there are a few inexpensive hostels here. This is a less expensive place to stay in, and it isn't as crowded and noisy as the city center.

This region is ideal for families, couples, and independent travelers. It's ideal for anyone who wants to see downtown Cork but doesn't want to pay the high prices associated with staying in the city center.

Top Highlights in the Victorian Quarter

- The Cork Opera House is the best spot to go in the Victorian Quarter to see a one-of-a-kind show.
- Cross the St. Patrick's Bridge for some of the greatest views of the Lee River.
- For some of the greatest meals in Cork, visit Greenes Restaurant or Isaacs Restaurant.
- Mother Jones Flea Market is a great place to pick up some local goods.

Where to Stay in the Victorian Quarter

Sheilas Tourist Hostel, popular among younger travelers, is arguably the most cheap location to stay in all of Cork. It's in the heart of the Victorian Quarter, and rates start at €18 ($21) per night.

If you wish to stay in a somewhat better spot, choose the Metropole Hotel Cork, which is close to some of the greatest stores in the Victorian Quarter. The nightly rate starts at €130 ($153).

Hotel Issacs Cork City is ideal for families and is positioned immediately next to Greenes Restaurant, only a 5-minute walk from the city center. The nightly rate starts at €115 ($135) and varies throughout the year.

Tivoli 4

Tivoli, a neighborhood east of Cork, is a lovely spot to stay directly on the river. This neighborhood is far less crowded than the others on this list, so it's a fantastic spot to stay if you want a bit more peace and quiet during your vacation.

This neighborhood might not have as much to offer, yet it is still worth visiting. It has a much more homey feel than the city itself, which might be a refreshing change to return to every evening for your lodging.

This neighborhood is ideal for all sorts of travelers, especially those looking for a calmer environment. It's particularly popular among couples looking for a peaceful break near Cork City.

Top Highlights in Tivoli

- Flemings Restaurant serves outstanding French cuisine.
- Watch the various shipping vessels arrive and depart on the River Lee at the Tivoli Docks.
- Visit Blackrock Pier and the Blackrock Castle Observatory for spectacular views and to see a stunning 16th-century castle.

Where to Stay in Tivoli

Spend the night at Flemings Country House for an extraordinary and one-of-a-kind experience. This fashionable spot, only 10 minutes from Cork's city center, is popular with couples, with prices starting at €111 ($130) per night.

Clayton Hotel Silver Springs is a lovely 4-star hotel with excellent views of the Lee River. It's located directly over the river from Blackrock Castle, and prices start at €111 ($130) per night.

The Belvedere Lodge, located inside an ancient Victorian building, is a lovely place to stay for a romantic getaway. Breakfast is included, and rates start at €99 ($116).

St. Luke's Cross 5

St. Luke's Cross, a suburb just outside of Cork, is another great place to stay if you don't want to stay in the city center. It's a short drive from Cork, although some buses travel between this neighborhood and the city center.

Though there isn't much to do at St. Luke's Cross, the neighborhood is home to reasonably priced lodging. It's also a college neighborhood, as Griffith College Cork is located just close to Cork Kent station.

Because it is close to the city center yet quieter, the St. Luke's Cross neighborhood is popular among families. It also has a far more rural atmosphere than the metropolitan life of Cork.

Top Highlights in St. Luke's Cross

- Explore Griffith College Cork's campus to discover some stunning architecture.
- For a good time, listen to some live music at Live at St. Luke's.
- The best pub in St. Luke's Cross is John Henchy & Sons, which serves classic pub fare.

Where to Stay in St. Luke's Cross

The Address Cork, also known as the Ambassador Hotel & Health Club, is a beautiful 19th-century hotel with stunning views of Cork's skyline. It also houses McGettigan's Cookhouse & Bar, where prices begin at €114 ($134).

The Montenotte Hotel is one of the best locations to stay in Cork City and is ideal for families or couples on a romantic break. Rates start at €162 ($190), but what makes this hotel so special is that they provide apartment room choices, which are ideal for longer visits.

Cork is a fantastic destination to visit whether you are traveling alone, with family, or with a loved one! Whatever sort of traveler you are, Cork has a neighborhood that will meet your demands and budget. Fortunately, the local bus will connect you to the city center regardless of the neighborhood you select for your vacation to Cork. Have a great vacation!

Best Luxury Hotels

Where To Stay And Best Luxury Hotels In Cork

If you're considering visiting Cork, or better yet, indulging in Cork, then this section will help you learn about the fanciest and swankiest hotels in the area. You have the choice of staying in Cork City or venturing farther west for some harsh countryside to complement your opulent lifestyle. Whether you take the scenic road or remain in the city, you won't have to sacrifice the finer things in life.

As a side note, to make your stay as nice as possible, pick up some artisan chocolates from The English Market to nibble on in your presidential suite. At that point, make arrangements for private tours wherever you go. The Blarney Stone, Cork City Gaol, and any walking excursions. Whatever you want to call it. Nothing says "I'm worth it" like having your own personal chaperone. But first, we need to find out where we're going to stay...

Fota Island Resort and Spa

At Fota Island Resort and Spa, there is enough to do. For starters, it's directly next to Fota Island Wildlife Park, one of Cork's most popular attractions. The hotel features three golf courses, a luxury spa, an indoor pool, and a fine dining restaurant. The resort's whole foundation is centered on "personal energy, vitality, holistic relaxation, and pampering"

In terms of lodging, guests have the option of staying in either self-catering lodges or hotel suites. The design is subdued and drab throughout, so picture cushy carpets, non-patterned linens, and a muted grey color palette. Personally, I'd aim to secure a larger apartment on the top floor so that I could have a good view of the rolling countryside from my gigantic, floor-to-ceiling windows.

Hayfield Manor

Hayfield Manor is a five-star luxury boutique hotel in Cork City. The Scally family runs it, and the accommodations vary from "superior rooms" and "grand suites" to the even more expensive "master suite." There are no bedsits in this area. The suite bathrooms are marbled with gold fittings, the lobby boasts a roaring fire and deep-set couches, and there's even a terrace where you can dine al fresco.

Speaking of restaurants, Hayfield Manor has quite a few. There's the laid-back Manor Bar, Perrot's Garden Bistro, elegant dining at Orchid, a private dining room, a Vine Wine Cellar, and the Boole Suite. There's also a well-equipped health spa with Elemis treatments and an indoor pool. What an amazing site! Wear your finest jewelry and come down here for a couple of nights.

Castlemartyr Resort Hotel

Castlemartyr is a small village of 500 people in south Cork that was constructed in 1210 by The Knights Templar. The Knights Templar was a Christian military order from the time of the Crusades. By the 17th century, Castlemartyr had constructed a splendid manor house atop it, which now serves as this ritzy, five-star hotel.

There are family-friendly accommodations, presidential suites, manor staterooms, and more options for lodging. You can expect nothing less than opulence here, with four-poster beds, sitting rooms, objets d'art, and an abundance of sumptuous linens. In addition, visitors have access to an indoor pool, a fantastic spa, a gym, and a golf course. The resort is also within a 30-minute drive from Cork International Airport. So, if you're looking for a respite from your tough job in the most spectacular way, consider this as your sign!

Vienna Woods Hotel

Vienna Woods is located on the outskirts of Cork City, atop the Glashaboy River. The rural home was erected in 1756, but it currently boasts a brilliant mustard-toned facade (impossible to miss, even though it's nestled away in Glanmire's forests). The former owner, Joan Shubuek, adopted the name "Vienna" in 1964 because the surroundings reminded her of her native Austria.

If you like "bohemian luxe" décor, you'll like the decor as a premium visitor. As a result, there are a lot of yellow, purple, and teal splashes of color throughout, as well as unusual patterned wallpaper, Chinoiserie vases, and chandeliers. Because of the glass atrium and abundance of metal fixtures, the area is overall incredibly bright and airy. Meanwhile, the dining room is decorated in an Art Nouveau style. Perfect design! Vienna Woods is thus ideal for well-established creatives who like eclectic luxury.

Maryborough Hotel & Spa

Maryborough is another regency manor home in the Cork area. It's nearly 300 years old and has plenty of charm! To get the most out of your time here, I recommend reserving the Master Suite, which is the most luxurious and spectacular suite, with views of the garden from the balcony. I also want to imagine myself in this suite, wearing a plush robe and slippers, ordering room service, and exuding a top-tier air.

There are also fantastic package offers available for couples (a great option for upcoming anniversaries or honeymoons). One of these options includes a bottle of champagne brought to your room upon arrival. It also includes a four-course meal at Bellini's Restaurant with a bottle of house wine and a 50-minute spa treatment at their health club. Winner!

Liss Ard Estate

The Liss Ard Estate is a Georgian rural manor home with an AA rating. It is located in the ever-popular West Cork town of Skibbereen. Despite its historic status, the interiors are modern, warm, and light, with a hint of Scandinavian style.

Aside from the usual services, the hotel also provides a picnic service, with a basket full of afternoon goodies to enjoy on the grounds. You may take this and contemplate gravity like Isaac Newton beneath one of their oak trees. If that doesn't work, you may eat seasonally at their upmarket restaurant or have afternoon tea in the sitting room with the newspaper. If you want to spoil your honey, this is the place to go.

The Castle Townshend

The Castle Hotel is a little difficult to find, mainly because of its general name... But as you learn more about it, you'll be glad you did. To begin with, this boutique hotel provides stunning views of the local port. Because the castle is directly on the water's edge, you'll be able to hear the waves from your window every morning.

The house has been in the family since the 1650s, and they've been entertaining visitors for 60 years - so they don't screw about. They understand what premium hospitality entails. The majority of the medieval elements, such as oak-paneled walls, vintage furnishings, family portraits in gilded frames, and wall tapestries, have been retained by the hotel. Each chamber, such as "The Gun Room" and "The Archbishop's Room," has a different theme (two rooms with the most character). If you consider luxury as "castles, rich hues, and regalia," The Castle Hotel in Castletownshend is the place for you.

The Montenotte Hotel

The Montenotte was formerly the house of a merchant prince in the 18th century. It has now been converted into a sleek and contemporary hotel with views of Cork City. It's a more modern and sleek option than the others, but it's likely to appeal to a wide range of people.

The hotel has an indoor pool, a luxurious elevated patio, and a fantastic bar and restaurant. On the premises, they even have a private cinema! If you want to enjoy the high life, make a reservation.

Oriel House

Oriel House is perhaps the least opulent on the list, but it still features luxury options, and the prices reflect this. In the mornings, you enjoy a slap-up breakfast and a lounge where you can read the newspaper or catch up on the news.

Imperial Hotel Cork City

The Imperial Hotel in Cork is located in the city, but it is also close to major sites such as Fota Island Wildlife Park, one of the city's primary attractions. The hotel itself is modern and meticulously decorated. In addition, they feature a magnificent luxury spa, a pool, and a fine dining restaurant.

A stay here will undoubtedly meet all of your luxury requirements! While you're at it, keep in mind that Cork is also excellent for traditional Irish cuisine. As a result, I recommend consulting this list of dishes to eat in Ireland and applying the information while ordering from a menu in Cork.

Best Boutique Hotels

Cork, the seat of County Cork and the second-largest city in Ireland, has an outstanding selection of hotels accessible to rent. Cork's greatest hotels are scattered around the city, but you'll never be far from the big attractions no matter where you stay.

In the city center, there are several five-star luxury hotels near St Patrick's Strip (Cork's main thoroughfare and a major retail street), with the best giving beautiful riverfront views (try the elevated north bank for the finest views!).

In calmer regions like Shandon (home to the famed Bells of Shandon) and the suburbs around Fitzgerald Park and University College Cork, there are charming guesthouses and eccentric stores.

If you want to venture farther afield, County Cork has a plethora of wonderful accommodation alternatives. On adjacent Fota Island, you'll find a one-of-a-kind hotel and spa, while in the nearby countryside, you'll find refurbished country manors and ancient estates that have been turned into world-class luxury spa hotels.

The Kingsley Hotel

The Kingsley Hotel is a four-star boutique hotel located in the city's calm western sector, near University College Cork. The riverbank setting is exceptional, and they even offer a one-of-a-kind "Pedals and Picnic Package" that encourages visitors to explore the lush suburbs on the hotel's bicycles. The nicest suites at The Kingsley Hotel have stunning views of the River Lee, and all are expertly furnished in soothing caramel-chocolate tones and outfitted with king-sized mattresses and premium bath items by Happy Buddha Rituals. .

In addition, the hotel features a limited number of luxury flats with two or three bedrooms and fully equipped kitchens. You can participate in fitness classes at the Health Club or simply go to the gym or swimming pool whenever you want. The spa has a luxurious thermal room, as well as a variety of calming spa services such as massages and facials.

The Montenotte Hotel

The Montenotte Hotel's stunning Panorama Bistro and Terrace, where you may wine and dine on a tall perch overlooking the northern bank of the River Lee, will take your breath away.

This heated outdoor terrace overlooks the Victorian Gardens and provides one of the greatest views in Cork for afternoon tea, drinks, breakfast, brunch, lunch, or supper. However, eating is only one incentive to stay at one of Cork's greatest hotels.

This four-star boutique hotel is housed within the ancient stone walls of an 18th-century merchant's mansion and offers luxury cinema screenings at the Cameo Cinema as well as the ultimate pampering experience at the Bellevue Spa.

The bright and colorful rooms rely on the building's Georgian-era heritage, but they're fully contemporary with all the amenities you'll need. All boutique rooms include king-size mattresses, unique Mark Buxton products, quality linen and soft bedclothes, and a private balcony. The nicest rooms provide spectacular views of Cork, luxurious bathrooms, and a welcome platter full of treats!

Imperial Hotel Cork City

The Imperial Hotel Cork City is only a four-minute walk from St Patrick's Street, making it impossible to find a more conveniently positioned hotel during your time in Cork. This four-star boutique hotel is also one of the top hotels in Cork, and you'll adore the luxurious accommodations, exquisite cuisine, and superb spa.

Since its inception in 1816, the Imperial Hotel Cork City has been a steadfast icon. This ancient hotel has been greeting visitors, travelers, celebrities, and politicians to Cork for over two centuries, and each room has a rich history.

For example, Room 115, the Michael Collins Suite was where Michael Collins, a senior revolutionary in the Irish War of Independence, spent his final night before being lain in an ambush in 1922. You'll be staying in Cork's most historic hotel if you book a boutique room here.

The deluxe apartments are furnished with timeless antiques and antiquated amenities (such as wind-up telephones) that add to the nostalgic atmosphere.

The rooms are similarly modern, with King Koil beds, Netflix and Disney, and J.J. Darboven coffee capsule machines (similar to a nicer Nespresso machine!).

After you've settled in, visit the Escape Spa for Aveda and Voya massages, as well as an aqua body polish and a signature facial. There are several showers and grottos in this spa, including scent and salt grottos, as well as tropical, mist, and rain showers.

There is a wide variety of eating alternatives to pick from. Sketch serves a traditional afternoon tea, followed by nighttime drinks and late-night charcuterie platters. Thyme, located at 76 on the Mall, has a sustainable concept and serves fine dining cuisine cooked with locally sourced ingredients and seasonal fruit.

Hayfield Manor

Remember what we said in the last section? Now learn the complete tale of Hayfield Manor.

Hayfield Manor's iconic red-brick front is complemented by a beautiful green facade of natural vines and trellis. This five-star hotel is one of the best boutique hotels in Cork, and a stay in one of the hotel's super-luxurious rooms will make you feel like a country lady or gentleman.

This country house is rather unique, given its proximity to the city center in the University College Cork neighborhood. It was formerly the residence of the Musgraves, a wealthy Corkonian mercantile family who purchased the property in the 1800s. It was later purchased by the Scally family, who transformed it into Cork's first five-star hotel in 1996. Hayfield Manor's "Manor Rooms" are the pinnacle of luxury.

The design is bright and contemporary, yet there are subtle hints of 19th-century grandeur that you won't find anywhere else. The king-size mattresses are ergonomically designed, and the marbled baths are just stunning. Upgrade to a "Historic Collections Suite" for more space and pleasures in a magnificent suite inspired by local history.

One of Cork's greatest spas is located at Hayfield Manor. When you experience the therapeutic joys of an Elemis deep tissue massage or a Ground Wellbeing Restorative Ritual, you'll understand why the Boutique Spa is sometimes booked weeks in advance. Enjoy a massage or a facial, then cool off in the spa pool before indulging in a Hayfield Manor Afternoon Tea.

Reserve a table at Perrotts Garden Bistro, a 2 AA Rosette restaurant located in the hotel's conservatory, for a leisurely lunch or supper. Book a table at Orchid's Restaurant, which overlooks the hotel's private gardens, for a more formal dining experience.

The Metropole Hotel

The Metropole Hotel, located in Cork's Victorian Quarter on the northern bank of the River Lee, is one of the city's oddest boutique hotels. This four-star hotel is colorful and historic, and you'll appreciate the fact that they're now commemorating almost 125 years of world-class service!

The hotel initially opened in 1897 and has since been a favorite of celebrities and even kings. In the early twentieth century, Walt Disney and John Steinbeck stayed here, and King Edward VII is claimed to have sipped tea on the rooftop.

You may follow in the footsteps of royalty by enjoying afternoon tea in the hotel's designated Tea Room, where you can swap the tea for prosecco if you're feeling extra festive. The MET, the hotel's upscale restaurant, serves brunch, lunch, and supper, while the hotel's bar hosts some of the top jazz performances during Cork's famed Jazz Festival every October.

The rooms are also fantastic, with a warm yet modern decor that encourages relaxation and well-being during your stay. Upgrade to a suite for the ultimate metropole experience, complete with antique furnishings and one-of-a-kind artwork in the hotel's most historic rooms.

Fota Island Hotel and Spa

When you book a stay at the Fota Island Hotel and Spa, you can enjoy the opulent comforts of a private island just 15 minutes from Cork.

This one-of-a-kind five-star hotel and spa is set on 780 acres of natural splendor on Fota Island, complete with sculpted gardens, forest walks, a wildlife park, and an 18-hole championship golf course.

This is the pinnacle of exclusivity in Cork, and the hotel's 131 deluxe rooms will keep you in top comfort. The soft carpets, clean linens, six-foot-long king-size Respa Beds, and Prija Toiletries in the luxury en-suite bathrooms will delight you.

The nicest rooms have wonderful views from private balconies, and if you want total isolation, book one of the hotel's self-catering island cabins.

Guests may make use of the fully-equipped Fota fitness facility, as well as the relaxing delights of the spa's hydrotherapy pool and heated mosaic loungers. There's a large indoor swimming pool (of course, heated), as well as massages, facials, a hammam session, and other refreshing spa services.

Cedric Bottarlini, Executive Head Chef, administers three restaurants at the Fota Island Hotel & Spa. The Amber Lounge provides afternoon tea, drinks, and a respectable 75-whiskey collection. The chilled-out Clubhouse serves handcrafted pizzas, grilled meats, and seafood, while The Cove's 10-serving Tasting Menu is a fine dining voyage of foraged delicacies and seasonal freshness.

Maryborough Hotel & Spa

If you want to experience the life of the Georgian nobility, a stay at the Maryborough Hotel & Spa is long overdue. This grandiose manor home, which dates back to 1710, is one of Cork's most historic properties.

This hotel is rich in history, and you'll like the historical features and furnishings, not to mention the 300-year-old listed gardens that you may explore at your leisure. In reality, there are 18 acres of grounds to explore in Douglas, a tranquil neighborhood just south of Cork's city center.

Bright views from the terrace or balcony, luxurious king mattresses, hypoallergenic linen, and silky soft bathrobes and slippers are all available in the rooms. What more would you expect from a four-star boutique hotel than high-end ESPA products in the luxury bathrooms?

If you enjoy ESPA products, you'll have a great day at the spa. ESPA products and treatments, as well as an outstanding thermal suite and spa pool, are at the top of the spa program. After a soothing swim, enjoy afternoon tea in the Garden Room, which overlooks the manor home and is served on bone china plates.

Don't eat too many cucumber sandwiches, though, because you'll want to save space for dinner at Bellini's, a 2 AA Rosette restaurant with an art deco theme. On the dinner menu, you'll find Irish beef, Slaney lamb, and Dover sole, while in the mornings, this is where you can fuel up with a full Irish breakfast.

Cork's Vienna Woods Hotel & Villas

Escape the city by staying at Cork's Vienna Woods Hotel & Villas, a four-star boutique hotel on the banks of the Glashaboy River, just a 15-minute drive from the city.

This luxurious hotel is housed in an 18th-century country house, yet you'll appreciate how the property has been expertly modernized while retaining its original Georgian charm. Large windows and high ceilings add to the impression of openness in the rooms, which are bright and colorful.

However, if you want room for up to eight individuals, toasty underfloor heating, and a fully fitted kitchen, consider upgrading to a self-catering villa!

This family-run boutique stay has 22 acres of private gardens and forests for you to explore, as well as convenient access to nearby golf courses (there are several) and walking paths.

On the grounds, you may have a magnificent afternoon tea, while Mabel Crawfords Bistro provides exquisite local food in a historic setting. Many historic characteristics from the 150-year-old kitchen, where it still cooks, have been preserved, including exposed brickwork and a traditional open fire and hearth.

The Dean Cork

The Dean Cork is one of Cork's newest and most exciting hotels. In fact, we'd go so far as to claim that this is the coolest hotel in Cork, with a rooftop bar and restaurant, digital nomad offices, and a modern style and décor that few other boutique hotels can equal!

Also, there's a very amazing relaxation pool with the feel of a Roman-style bath, not to mention a sauna, steam room, and power gym where you can work up a sweat.

But you'll want to check in before using the wonderful amenities, even if you're tempted by the Marshall amplifiers, Samsung smart screens (with Netflix, of course), and SMEG refrigerators (well stocked with loads of sweets, presumably) that come standard in every room. Add super-crisp bed sheets, a strong rainforest shower, a Nespresso machine, and other amenities, and you've got yourself a winner.

The Dean Bar, a sophisticated café and bar on the ground level, provides coffee in the morning and drinks in the evening. Head to the fifth story for panoramic views of Cork and supper and drinks on the rooftop terrace at Sophie's Restaurant.

The Address Cork

The Address Cork is one of the nicest hotels in Cork, and you'll instantly fall for the Victorian nostalgia prevalent throughout this four-star facility.

The Address Cork began as a hospital in the 1870s and was turned into a premium boutique hotel in 2013. It was renamed The Address Cork in 2020, yet the hotel has kept much of its 19th-century charm. The outside is fashioned in the era's typical red-brick architecture, with wrought iron verandas, bay and bow windows, and a sense of timelessness.

When you enter your boutique room, you'll see the high vaulted ceilings, but you'll also notice the modern conveniences, such as comfortable bedding, high-speed Wi-Fi, and premium amenities. The Address Cork is well placed on the slopes above the northern bank of the River Lee, and the best suites give spectacular views of the city from private balconies.

The River Lee Hotel

Cork's most distinctive natural feature is the River Lee, and there's no better location to stay than along its famed banks. The River Lee, a beautiful four-star boutique resort giving outstanding views of the water through large floor-to-ceiling windows, is one of the greatest riverside hotels in Cork.

Every luxury accommodation at The River Lee Hotel has stunning panoramic windows, and you'll also enjoy the views from the hotel's riverside restaurant and bar's outdoor (but underground) terrace. During the day, the River Club provides breakfast and lunch, and in the evening, it serves small meals and beverages. Inside the Grill Room, you may have a more substantial supper of steak or seafood in a very stylish environment.

The River Lee's rooms are similarly stylish, with colorful designs and luxurious furniture (oh did we mention the views?). The leisure facilities are also first-rate, with a 20-meter indoor swimming pool, sauna, steam room, and fully-equipped gym available to all visitors.

Gabriel House Guesthouse

Why not book a boutique room at Gabriel House Guesthouse if you're seeking a pleasant stay in the city? This lovely, luxurious hotel has been greeting tourists to Cork since 1926, so you can be confident that they know a thing or two about providing excellent service!

The structure comes from the early twentieth century, and you'll enjoy historical elements like vaulted ceilings and antique furnishings during your stay. You'll like the hotel's high setting on the north bank of the Lee River.

Rooms provide beautiful views of the hotel's private gardens, where you may unwind after a day of touring in the city. The garden is also quite practical (it houses herbs, vegetables, and animals), and you'll watch the hotel's chickens laying the eggs you'll be eating at breakfast.

The hotel's ecological focus includes homegrown eggs and vegetables. They also supply electric car chargers, and their energy is virtually entirely derived from solar power.

If you're looking for one-of-a-kind hotels in Cork, the Gabriel House Guesthouse may be your best choice!

Best Budget-Friendly Hotels

Cork Airport Hotel

Cork Airport Hotel is a five-minute walk from Cork Airport terminal and offers contemporary and spacious rooms at a reasonable price. The Olivio Bar & Restaurant serves some of the tastiest pizzas in town, touting authentic Italian cuisine made with locally sourced ingredients. Every morning, a continental buffet breakfast of fresh bread, pastries, cold meats, and more is served, and a grab-and-go option is available beginning at 4 a.m. if you have an early departure.

Vienna Woods, Glanmire

You'll feel a world away from the center of Cork when you're high up on a steep hill surrounded by trees, even if you're just 3 miles (5 kilometers) away. It was originally designed as a hunting lodge and preserves its medieval charm while being adequately contemporary, having undergone a multimillion-euro refurbishment. Each of the hotel's 48 guest rooms, five suites, and eight vacation cottages is individually decorated with brocade wallpaper, and the head chef creates surprising flavors and odd combinations in the kitchen.

Belvedere Lodge

This quaint family-run guesthouse has been lovingly designed with color accents and is nestled among its serene grounds complete with cascades, ponds, and a gazebo. The highlight of the show is a typical Irish breakfast, so load up on scrambled eggs, smoked salmon, mushrooms, and grilled tomato, all prepared to order. Rooms contain all the necessities - in the summer, choose a room with an exclusive entrance to the grounds for an extra unique touch.

Blarney Castle Hotel

This is a wonderful alternative for budget-conscious travelers who don't want to sacrifice location. It's about 200 yards (180 meters) from Blarney Castle. Locals arrive early for the traditional cooked breakfasts and remain late for fantastic Irish music and cool ales at Johnny's Bar. Ingredients for your meals are acquired locally, and customers rave about the monkfish served with sun-flushed tomatoes and sautéed potatoes. And, while the rooms are basic, they are not lacking in comfort.

Jurys Inn Cork

The Jurys provide all the necessities for a comfortable stay without the expensive additions. The beds are comfy, the sheets are fresh, and you will receive complimentary amenities as well as free WiFi. Whether you're here for business or pleasure, this is an ideal location if you want to spend most of your time out and about; take advantage of the central position near Cork railway station. It's an excellent choice for a low-cost hotel in Cork.

The Clayton Hotel

Whether for business or leisure, our charming riverbank hotel is well-located to allow you to enjoy the best that the city has to offer. Its 198 spacious guest rooms have 32-inch televisions, in-room safes, complimentary Wi-Fi, and a free-standing ironing board with iron, while the hotel's 18m (60ft) pool with sauna and hot tub is where you'll want to unwind after a long day.

Cork International Hotel

While staying at an airport hotel isn't the most exciting proposition, Cork International is quite luxurious for what might easily be another terrible motorway motel. This hotel is scarcely option B, with modern yet pleasant guest rooms and a location only 10 minutes from the city center. Are you awaiting a flight?

The Metropole Hotel

The Metropole, built-in 1897 but with modern ensuite bathrooms and premium Karre products, is a historic hideaway close to stores, boutiques, pubs, and diners. Join the locals in the vibrant Met bar for a drink, while Sundays are reserved for Brunch in the City, where you can indulge in great breakfast classics washed down with free-flowing prosecco.

Best Places to Stay in Cork to Get Around on Foot

Maldron Hotel South Mall Cork City

This upmarket hotel has a bar/lounge, coffee shop/café, and snack bar/deli, all of which are ideal for getting a bite to eat. Other guests praise the excellent bedding and convenient location. When you're ready to unwind, come to the terrace for a drink.

Bru Bar & Hostel

This is where I stayed when I visited Cork and would suggest it to anyone trying to save money. It's clean and comfy, plus it's in a convenient location. It also features a pool table and a great social atmosphere for single travelers.

CHAPTER FIVE

Famous Local Dishes and Drinks to Try in CORK

Cork is an excellent place to sample Irish food and drink. Make sure to try some of the regional favorites, such as:

Murphy's Stout

This well-known Irish stout is made in Cork.

Skirts and Kidneys

Skirts and Kidneys is a substantial stew made with pig skirts (backbone and rib trimmings), kidneys, potatoes, onions, and water. The stew is seasoned with white pepper, salt, and thyme, and maize flour is frequently used to thicken it.

The dish is a specialty of Cork, which was a significant supplier of preserved beef and pig to the British Armed Forces, thus enormous quantities of offal were always readily accessible. It is suggested that the meal be served with some crusty bread on the side.

Durrus

Durrus is an Irish semi-soft cheese made from raw cow's milk. It's been made in West Cork's Coomkeen Valley since 1979. The cheese has a pinkish-colored naturally washed rind. There is a straw-colored paste beneath it with several irregular tiny eyeballs spread across it.

When young (10 days), the texture is smooth and flexible, and the tastes range from green, mellow, and mild to robust, deep, and earthy when ripe (5-8 weeks). Durrus is best paired with beer, prosecco, champagne, or medium-bodied red wines.

Dubliner

Dubliner is a kind of Irish cheese made in County Cork. Cow's milk is used to make the cheese. It has a hard, smooth, and crystalline texture, with tastes that are nutty, crisp, and sweet. Dubliner has a natural rind and is available in a variety of flavors nowadays.

John Lucey developed the cheese, and he still preserves the secret formula. The Dubliner is best paired with Cabernet or a pint of Guinness beer. It can also be melted between pieces of crusty brown bread.

Spiced Beef

Although it is traditionally consumed on Christmas and New Year's Eve in County Cork, spiced beef is available all year in specialty shops throughout Ireland. Its simplicity is likely surpassed only by its duration, which can take up to a month or two in some situations.

A rump or silverside beef joint is salted and marinated in spices and saltpeter for a few days, and in some circumstances, weeks. After curing, the meat is cooked in water or stout and possibly baked.

Coolea

Coolea is a cow's milk Gouda-style cheese created by the Willems family in County Cork since 1979. The cheese has a hard, crumbly, and robust structure beneath its waxy exterior coating. Coolea is buttery and mild in flavor while young, but as it ages (up to 18 months), it acquires sweet and caramel-like flavors with visible protein crystals.

The cheese is available in three varieties: young Coolea (3 months), mature Coolea (12 months), and extremely mature Coolea (18 months). It is suggested that it be used in mac and cheese, with potatoes, or in a grilled cheese sandwich.

Blarney Castle

Blarney Castle is an Irish cheese named after the city of Blarney, which is located near Cork. The cheese is created from grass-fed cow milk. It has a golden yellow hue, a semi-soft and creamy texture, and mild and acidic tastes.

Many people compare Blarney Castle cheese to young Gouda, so serve it with fresh fruit and a glass of crisp wine on the side, such as Sauvignon Blanc.

Fish & Chips

Nothing beats a great meal of fish and chips on a sunny day. While not native to Ireland, the basic fish and chips have become our unofficial national cuisine, and are served everywhere from the local chip shop to our most upscale restaurants.

Bacon & Cabbage

"I'm simply a savage about bacon and cabbage," says musician Brendan Shine, and we couldn't agree more! One of Ireland's most beloved dinners is this family favorite. For a genuine taste of Ireland, serve with a white parsley sauce.

Best Places to Visit in CORK

Blarney Castle: This historic castle is home to the Blarney Stone, which is claimed to offer anybody who kisses it the gift of gab. Even if you're afraid of heights, it's worth going to the castle's summit for the breathtaking views of the surrounding landscape.

English Market: For any foodie, this ancient market is a must-see. There's something for everyone with over 100 vendors providing anything from fresh fruit to cooked cuisine.

Cork City Gaol: A former jail turned tourist attraction. Visitors may learn about the prison's history and see the cells where many renowned Irish revolutionaries were previously imprisoned.

University College Cork (UCC) is one of Ireland's most attractive universities. Visitors may take a campus tour and visit some of the university's most famous monuments, including the Boole Library and the Campanile.

St. Fin Barre's Church: This magnificent cathedral is one of Cork's most recognizable monuments. The cathedral's stunning stained glass windows may be admired, and visitors can climb to the top of the tower for panoramic views of the city.

Spike Island in Cork Harbour is home to Charles Fort, a 17th-century star fort. Visitors may take a ferry to the island and see the gardens and structures of the fort.

Midleton Distillery: This distillery produces the world-famous Jameson Irish Whiskey. Visitors to the distillery may take a tour and learn about the whiskey-making process.

Fota Wildlife Park: This wildlife park is home to over 100 different animal species from throughout the world. Visitors can join a safari tour of the park or go around on their own.

Cobh: This ancient harbor town was the Titanic's final port of call before it perished in 1912. The Titanic Experience Cobh Museum teaches visitors about the Titanic's history.

Best Places to Eat in CORK City

Cork, Ireland's third biggest city, spans both sides of the River Lee and is known among locals as "the actual capital of Ireland." This is a vibrant, adventurous, and unpretentious city on the stunning Atlantic coast, as seen by the restored buildings, bustling culture, and outstanding art scene. The city is unquestionably Ireland's gourmet center, and here are ten of the top restaurants in Cork.

Café Paradiso

Café Paradiso, one of Cork's oldest enterprises, is a vegetarian venue that has become an institution in the city's eating scene. The café, which has garnered several prizes and acclaim over the years, blends ingredients and flavors in surprising ways, making each meal a delightful work of art.

Dennis Cotter, the venue's proprietor, has released four cookbooks as a result of its popularity. The 20-year-old restaurant is still hard to top, with a menu that is regularly created using fresh, seasonal ingredients, giving a vegetarian option that includes sushi, risotto with blood orange salad, beets and blue cheese, and couscous with feta and butternut squash pine nuts.

Quay Co-op

The Quay Co-op, located in a city center venue beside an in-house bakery and three stores offering organic foods, is another longtime business in Cork city, with light dining rooms, oak flooring, fireplaces, and enormous French windows overlooking the river Lee.

High-quality vegetarian and gluten-free products, a unique technique of cooking, a buzzy, vibrant ambiance, and friendly, good-natured personnel never fail to delight newcomers and faithful customers of the 30-year-old restaurant.

The Farmgate Café

Farmgate Café is an excellent choice if you chance to be passing by Cork's busiest and most popular area, the English Market, for a terrific morning coffee, a tasty working lunch, or an afternoon tea.

The decision is between sitting in the dining room or on the balcony for the greatest goat's cheese sandwich in town or the wonderful lemon tart, enjoying the hustle and bustle of rush hour or the ambiance of the indoor market.

Every day, lunch options are chalked on the chalkboard, and desserts are delectably exhibited in the café window. Freshly made scones with jam or marmalade, granola and seasonal fruits, soups, chowders, specialized entrees, and beautiful pastries may all be enjoyed at the bustling marketplace.

Star Anise

Star Anise restaurant attracts a large number of guests due to its fresh Mediterranean food and courteous service. Virginie Sarraziny, the proprietor, is a French cook who grew up surrounded by fine cuisine and wine as a result of her chef father and wine-expert mother.

Carolyn Buckley, the head chef, honed her trade in Parisian restaurants, and her ravioli, gnocchi, and other delectable delicacies provide diners with a fantastic dining experience. With fantastic value meals, an unusual wine selection, and a casual and intimate ambiance, this is one of Cork's most dependable supper destinations.

Electric

Electric was founded on the idea of socializing via food and drink. The Electric, housed in a rebuilt art-deco edifice that was once a bank, soars above the Lee River, offering panoramic views of St Finbarr Cathedral. A lively bar below serves great cocktails, while a fish bar upstairs, dangling directly over the sea, is inspired by Portuguese and Spanish tavernas. If the weather permits, the large veranda gives stunning views of the river, complemented by delectable tapas and wine.

Flemings Restaurant

The spectacular medieval Georgian mansion, built on five acres of lawn and patio grounds, was purchased in 1989 by Michael and Eileen Fleming and is now home to Flemings, one of Cork's most elegant dining destinations. The lovely mansion with its original characteristics, built by famous merchants on a hill overlooking the eastern part of Cork, is an outstanding site for any event, from intimate lunches to wedding festivities.

The menu is appropriately French, using local, fresh ingredients, and is served in the French Empire-style dining room with plush chairs and crystal chandeliers: monkfish served in red wine fish sauce, lamb with couscous, cheeses from local farms, and various delicious desserts offer high-quality dining at a reasonable price.

Market Lane

Market Lane, a vibrant corner bistro with a relaxed and pleasant environment, friendly service, and superb food, is widely regarded as one of Cork's top restaurants. Some of the items on an ever-changing menu include sweet potato and goat's cheese pastry, cod croquettes, tempura of monkfish with herb, and lemon potato cake with tomato, olive, and saffron ragout. The majority of the products are derived from neighboring English Market or local artisan producers, making Market Lane the ideal blend of high quality and outstanding value dining.

Blair's Inn

Blair's Inn ticks all the boxes for a wonderful cultural experience, with a classic Irish pub ambiance, homey food, artisan brews, live music sessions, and scenic surroundings. The Blair family owns and runs the bar, which is located just outside Blarney in County Cork and specializes in seafood and steaks. Shellfish and seafood are sourced from neighboring Kenmare, Angus steaks and sausages are sourced from local butchers, and artisan cheeses are created in County Clare creameries.

Sitting by the fire with a drink from a local microbrewery, a delicious supper, or singing along with traditional musicians in a great two-hour session will round off the Irish cultural experience.

Sage Restaurant

Sage Restaurant is the creation of young chef Kevin Aherne, and it serves five different meals per week, including the legendary '12-mile menu,' where every product is acquired within a 12-mile radius of the restaurant.

The restaurant is housed in a beautiful stone structure on the main street of Midleton, County Cork, and has modern surroundings furnished in light sage and cream, with wooden flooring and high-backed leather seats. Every meal is a creative blend of flavors: succulent beef, roast shoulder of pork with applesauce, and sweet red cabbage are just a few of the specialties.

The Coach House Bar and Restaurant

The Coach House Bar and Bistro in the Old Imperial Hotel in Youghal, County Cork, is a fantastic discovery for superb food, a pleasant atmosphere, quick service, and good value.

The Coach House, which impresses on every level, is a location where friendly local people of the little coastal town meet with visitors and tourists while eating local Irish products in tastefully furnished settings. Modern and imaginative meals are delivered in generous servings, and the cuisine pleases all palates. This is a popular restaurant, thus reservations are strongly advised.

Best Restaurants in CORK

There are some fantastic places to dine in Cork City, and many of the city's restaurants are as good as any of Ireland's gourmet hot spots.

The restaurants listed below are our picks for the best in Cork.

The SpitJack Cork

SpitJack Cork, which opened in 2017, is widely regarded as one of the greatest restaurants in Cork City. Everything focuses honey-baked on the rotisserie idea at this award-winning restaurant.

The restaurant exclusively employs the best local meats and veggies from the well-known English Market. The classic Italian rotisserie porchetta and the Ballycotton fish are also outstanding.

The codfish cake is very delicious. Order the honey-baked goat cheese salad if you prefer vegetarian fare. SpitJack Cork features a gorgeous interior design and great service in addition to substantial meals.

Jacobs on the Mall

Jacobs on the Mall, located in the center of Cork City, is a foodie's dream. This contemporary-style restaurant, which has received a Certificate of Excellence and multiple other distinctions, specializes in modern European cuisine presented in a romantic atmosphere.

Although this renowned Cork restaurant can seat over 150 people, reservations are required, especially on weekends. So, what's the deal here?

As an appetizer, I propose seared scallops with maple Baltimore bacon and pomme puree, and for the main course, roast pig belly with whipped chive potatoes.

They also have a fixed menu that is accessible all evening. Do you have a sweet tooth? Order the warm chocolate fudge cake topped with vanilla ice cream and chopped hazelnuts.

Strasbourg Goose

Strasbourg Goose is located in the heart of Cork, right off Patrick Street in a little pedestrian lane.

For the last 20 years or more, Triona and John (Head Chef) have owned this restaurant, which has a French atmosphere.

Their oven-roasted lamb shank, as well as the duck breasts, served with gratin potatoes, are to die for.

In addition to the amazing food, the restaurant has a wide wine selection that includes both local and foreign wines (there are also plenty of great pubs in Cork close by).

Elbow Lane Brew and Smoke House

For those who want superbly cooked meat, Elbow Lane Brew and Smoke House is perhaps one of the greatest places to eat in Cork City.

This magnificent restaurant is located in an L-shaped area with traditional décor and features an open-plan kitchen and a massive wood-fired barbecue. The cuisine is filling and delectable!

Sunchokes with hazelnuts make an excellent appetizer. Main courses such as pig neck and monkfish with lamb bacon are popular among hungry customers.

The incredible smokehouse sauce is what sets this business apart. Order the slow-smoked pork ribs with homemade coleslaw, roast sweet potatoes, and smokehouse sauce to see what I mean.

Quinlans Seafood Bar Cork

Quinlans Seafood Bar, located in the heart of Cork, specializes in fresh catch of the day and seafood. Everything ordered here is incredibly fresh because the seafood is delivered daily from the boats and prepared to order.

Whether you prefer prawns or crab, or local salmon or haddock, Quinlans' broad fish and seafood buffet has something for everyone.

The restaurant's batter is made according to a specific recipe. Those looking for a healthy choice will be pleased to learn that their order can be pan-fried in olive oil.

Liberty Grill

Is an excellent choice for a relaxed eating experience. What's for dinner? The restaurant serves burgers and steaks, as well as vegetarian cuisine and fish from the adjacent English Market.

Guests like the restaurant's all-day brunch menu, which includes staples like French toast and eggs benedict.

Get yourself here if you're looking for fantastic eateries in Cork City where the only thing better than the price is the flavor.

Market Lane

One of Cork City's most popular eateries is the award-winning Market Lane. They get their meat from the adjacent English Market, create their beer in a nearby brewery, and have a greenhouse where they cultivate their local veggies and fresh herbs.

Favorites include slow-cooked beef short rib in a sticky red wine and treacle sauce, roast turnips, and creamy mashed potatoes, roast marinated chicken, buttered root vegetables, braised red cabbage, and creamy mashed potatoes and gravy.

Sirloin steak may also be ordered, and all of the beef is Irish, locally produced, and matured for 28 days by the Allshire family in Rosscarbery.

Goldie

Goldie, one of Cork's newest additions to the restaurant industry, is a terrific spot to savor fish and seafood.

The restaurant has a large seafood menu with favorites including crab, langoustines, and scallops.

Pollock and megrim are perhaps less popular alternatives, but equally tasty, according to head chef Aisling Moore and executive chef Stephen Kehoe. Make sure to get their specialty craft beer from the sibling restaurant across the street.

CHAPTER SIX

The Best Bars, Clubs & Nightlife in CORK

Coughlan's Live

Coughlan's Live, located on Douglas Street, constantly draws a crowd with its extensive selection of music and comedy events.

Coughlan takes pleasure in giving tourists a wonderful experience, having hosted some of the best musicians from Ireland and throughout the world.

7 Douglas Street, Ballintemple, Cork, T12 DX39, Ireland

The Roundy

The Roundy is one of Cork's most renowned pubs, and a visit here is a must if you want to experience the legendary Cork nightlife in all its splendor.

With five nights of live music and comedy every week, a vibrant environment, and a diverse crowd, this is a must-stop on any Cork pub crawl.

1 Castle St, Center, Cork, T12 RX09, Ireland

Sin É

Sin É is well-known for its live music performances.
Sin É in Cork is the place to go for traditional Irish music sessions. Visitors and locals alike go to this famous neighborhood bar to see brilliant performers, drink up the pleasant ambiance, and have a tasty pint.

This is a must-visit pub in Cork for fresh Guinness and great craic.

Cork, T23 KF5N, Ireland, 8 Coburg St, Victorian Quarter

The Old Town Whiskey Bar at Bodega

What else can we say? This award-winning restaurant provides delicious meals every day, has Ireland's largest whiskey bar, and changes into a lively nightclub with a terrific audience at night.

The magnificent décor is only one of the numerous things that contribute to the allure of this Corkonian venue.

44-45 Cornmarket Street, Centre, Cork, T12 W27H, Ireland

Rearden's Pub

There's not much missing for your night out at Rearden's with food, sports, amazing beverages, and music.

Cork nightlife is at its finest here since it is the city's largest bar venue for live music and has a few distinct hubs where you can let your hair down, whether you want to dance the night away or socialize with the locals. Make sure you learn some Cork slang first!

26 Washington Street, Centre, Cork, T12 WNP8, Ireland
Sober Lane
Cork nightlife is all about having fun, and Sober Lane, one of the most iconic places to hang out in the city, offers a whole host of fun events every night of the week.

As well as being a lively gastropub, you can enjoy Tuesday quiz nights, energetic music, quirky events, and a wide range of beverages.

5 Sullivan's Quay, Cork, T12 H771, Ireland

Chambers Pub

Drag performances and karaoke are popular at Chambers Bar.

This all-time favorite LGBTQ+ pub in Cork's city center is the ideal location for a variety of thrilling nights and events.

Chambers caters to individuals seeking a great night out, featuring drag performances every Thursday through Sunday, karaoke, and so much more.

Washington Street, Centre, Cork, Ireland

A Bróg Bar with a Kitchen

Every night of the week, this regularly busy pub is the spot to soak up a terrific ambiance, mingle with an interesting crowd, and listen to sounds performed by prominent DJs.

In addition to a wide selection of beers and pub cuisine, the music here will keep you on the dance floor all night.

74 Oliver Plunkett Street, Centre, Cork, T12 FP28, Ireland

Costigan's Pub

Costigan's Pub has been in operation since 1849. Costigan's is a local and visitor favorite for a well-rounded experience that includes live music and delicious cocktails.

This establishment takes itself in having one of the largest gin selections in Ireland, and its live performances attract music fans every week between Sunday and Thursday.

11 Washington Street West, Center, Cork, T12 N768, Ireland

CHAPTER SEVEN

The Most Romantic Things to Do In CORK City

After a stressful summer, September is typically seen as a month to reset. The kids have returned to school, you've survived a hectic summer of nonstop events, and now it's time to take a deep breath and consider "What now?" One may argue that taking some time off for oneself and one's special someone is the finest way to reset and discover the answer to that question; a chance to reconnect after all the turmoil.

We've compiled a selection of the best Cork fun date ideas.

Thursday Date Nights At The Crawford Art Gallery

Whether it's a first date or a married couple, it's wonderful to do something different than the usual "dinner and drinks" choice, and what better way to do it than with a tour of the city's Crawford Art Gallery? You don't have to be into art to enjoy this one-hour tour guided by some of the gallery's most passionate guides. The best part is that admission is free.

Take In A Play At One Of The City's Many Theatres

Cork Arts Theatre, Everyman Palace Theatre, Cork Opera House... Regardless of the night of the week, you choose to come, you will be spoiled for choice with the variety on offer in our city's theatres—all of which are less than a 10-minute walk from our hotel.

Get Them Giggling At A Comedy Gig In City Limits Or The Roundy Bar

They say laughing is the greatest medicine, and if you're scared your jokes aren't up to standard, don't worry since Cork has a fantastic comedy scene. The City Limits Comedy Club at the end of our block and the Roundy Bar (yep, it's extremely round) upstairs are two of our favorite places to laugh our worries away.

Go Cycling The Greenway To Blackrock Castle

Active couples will enjoy renting bikes and riding to Blackrock Castle along the Greenway. It's a nice leisurely excursion, only 2km from our accommodation, and why not stop at Blackrock Castle later for some cosmic exploration? Alternatively, you may take the Greenway al Crosshaven, a port town that is one of Cork's best-kept secrets to the world's oldest yacht club.

Ardu Street Art Tour

Put on your running shoes, get a cup of coffee from our Red Bean Roastery, and go exploring the City's street art. There are seven murals that can be seen across the city. If you want to learn more about the artist, you may take a self-guided tour.

Fota Wildlife Park And Fota House And Gardens

A local favorite, getting up close and personal with some exotic creatures from across the world at Fota Wildlife Park is undoubtedly one of the greatest activities for couples. You won't even need to drive because a normal train will take you there in only 10 minutes. After that, visit Fota House for some afternoon tea before touring the beautiful gardens and arboretum.

Zero Gravity Float Experience

For couples who enjoy spas but want a more unique spa experience, float your worries away in a sensory deprivation tank. Floating is a safe and effective technique to alleviate stress, treat chronic and acute pain, and recuperate from physical activity or accidents, making it a fantastic opportunity to connect on a whole new level.

Walk Along The River Lee Banks, Fitzgerald's Park And Otter Trail

Nothing beats a stroll along the banks of the Lee before arriving at Fitzgerald's Park, which features a duck pond, sky garden, and rose garden. Keep an eye out for the local otter as well.

Blarney Castle And Gardens

Blarney Castle, perhaps Ireland's most popular tourist site, is about 7 kilometers from Hotel Isaacs. Climb the spiral staircase for breathtaking views of the surrounding countryside before daringly hanging from the battlements to obtain the gift of eloquence by kissing the renowned Blarney Stone. The castle is flanked by lush gardens and parks, which include a poison garden and a lake stroll.

Ballycotton Cliff Walk

Take your loved one on a relaxing cliff-walk along the immensely popular Ballycotton Cliff Walk in the picturesque seaside community of Ballycotton. What could be more romantic than fresh sea air, coastline vistas of Ballycotton Lighthouse, and a secret beach near the halfway point?

Pitch And Putt

There are several pitch and putt courses in Cork to select from. Blarney and Douglas are our particular favorites. Give them a chance.

Budget Things to do in CORK City

Visit Passage West Maritime Museum in Cork

The Museum's collection includes maritime history, shipbuilding and ship repair, emigration, the US Navy presence in Cork Harbour, and the memories of generations of seafarers affiliated with the town.

While the Museum's primary focus is the past of Passage West and its link to the sea, future displays will highlight other parts of local history such as the Cork Blackrock & Passage Railway, folklife, fishing, rowing, social and political history, and notable local people.

The museum entry fee is €4.00 per person. Group pricing is negotiable, so contact them to work something out.

Passage West currently has a permanent location to store and show a wide range of unique artifacts and archive material collected across the town as well as surrounding Glenbrook, Monkstown, and the overall lower harbor region.

Titanic Experience in County Cork

Visit Cobh town and participate in an interactive experience to learn what life was like onboard the Titanic for many of the passengers. Cobh was the Titanic's final port of call, and on this guided tour, you will experience everything as it was, from the living rooms to the tragedy of the sinking ship. A one-of-a-kind cinematographic experience brings the entire adventure to life.

Immerse yourself in history at Titanic Experience Cobh, the last point of departure before the iconic ship tragically sank.

You begin your journey by checking in and collecting your boarding card, which contains the information for one of the 123 passengers who departed from Cobh. After the guided tour, you have approximately 30 minutes to explore the exhibition area, which is filled with interactive displays and audio-visual performances.

Learn about the circumstances that led up to the catastrophe, the findings of the British and American investigations, and the recovery of the wreckage. At the end of your adventure, you will learn if your traveler, as well as all of the other passengers from Cobh, survived the incident. This stunning experience should not be missed, so add the Titanic Experience Cobh to your Stack now! Adult € 11.00 Child € 7.50 Student/Senior | € 9.50

Monday – Sunday 10:00 – 17:30Monday - Sunday 10:00 - 17:30
Adult € 11.00 Child € 7.50 Student/Senior | € 9.50

Visit Leahy's Open Farm in Cork

The obstacle course is a great challenge for older kids; it takes a lot of balance, coordination, and talent to get through without falling. Leahy's Open Farm has a brand new Digger Park. This is one of the first opportunities for children to operate a real JCB mini digger. Make your way through the little forests, which are home to many animals and birds, until you reach the Beehives. The maze is a little under one acre in area, making it one of Ireland's biggest mazes.

A 9-hole golf course may appear easy, but there are so many obstacles in your path that it is a true struggle even for the most daring golfers. It is excellent fun for all ages. You may ride the quad and barrel train rides. This is also a lot of fun for the parents.

This massive structure holds the indoor go-kart track, slides and tunnels, sandpit, basketball hoop, rings, and much more... Even after all of the running about and activities at the farm, children appear to have enough energy to bounce around in the play barn, giving adults a respite to have a cup of coffee for a bit.

The farm's general entry ticket is €11.50 and is good for four hours. Children under the age of two are admitted free of charge.

Visit the Independence Museum in Kilmurry

Throughout the Rising, the War of Independence, and the Civil War, the village of Kilmurry was a hub of rebel activity. That same resolve, along with over a decade of volunteer labor and perseverance, has culminated in the establishment of the Independence Museum Kilmurry.

The new museum will serve as a historical and recreational focus for the Lee Valley and West Cork communities. Kilmurry's closeness to Kilmichael, Béal na Bláth, Crossbarry, and other War of Independence locations places it in a unique position to convey our country's past throughout the centennial decade.

The collection contains, among other things, the wheel from the Crossley Tender used in the Kilmichael Ambush, a man-trap used to snare poachers, Tom Barry's suitcase, and Terence MacSwiney artifacts.

You've come to the right place! Admission to the museum is absolutely free, although any gift is greatly appreciated.

Members of the Kilmurry Historical and Archaeological Association (KHAA) approached Theo Dahlke, curator of Allihies Copper Mine Museum on the Beara Peninsula and co-founder of Heritageworks, five years ago.

Theo had led the design and build of that award-winning exhibition and the committee from Kilmurry wanted to see how they might bring their own story to life in a similar way.

Theo stated "They are an incredibly tenacious bunch of people. There's a movement afoot in this country, where people are reclaiming their heritage at a local level, and we are privileged to work with people like the KHAA." KHAA Chairman, Noel Howard said "We felt that a museum would make Kilmurry a destination for the ever-growing number of history buffs and contribute to the economic and social development of our village... Heritage works have been a critical component in the creation and development of our new exhibition"

Visit the Old Cork Waterworks Experience in Cork

Old Cork Waterworks, built to service an empire at a time of revolt, maritime trade, and huge emigration, stands strong on the Cork hillside overlooking the River Lee and commanding the western approaches to Cork City. Our refurbished Victorian structures provide a Visitor Experience, Primary Science education space, Corporate Hire, and Conference amenities.

You've come to the right place! The center is open 24 hours a day, seven days a week. The hours of operation are 9:00 to 17:00.

The Old Cork Waterworks Experience provides a warm and courteous welcome, ensuring that your stay is memorable and pleasurable. Discover Cork's Heritage by Traveling Through Victorian Architecture Explore our exhibition area and unwind with a coffee in our spacious courtyard. There is free parking on-site.

€3.00 for children, €5.00 for adults

€15.00 for a family of two (2 adults and two children).

Senior citizens - €4.00

Students pay €4.00.

Visit the Blackrock Castle Observatory in Cork

A visit to Blackrock Castle Observatory, housed in an iconic Cork monument dating back to 1582, includes admission to Journeys of Exploration. This unique interactive experience takes visitors inside the heart of the Castle, telling the narrative of Cork's fortified terrain, commercial commerce, and the smugglers and pirates who sailed one of the world's deepest natural harbors. The tale is recounted through audio and guided tours of the 16th-century fort's gunnery, riverbank terrace, and towers.

The admission fee of €20 includes entry to the award-winning scientific center at MTU Blackrock Castle Observatory, a tour of the 16th-century castle, and a live astronomy display.

Visit Baltimore Castle in Cork

Baltimore Castle, also known as DÙN NA SÉAD, is a privately owned 13th-century Hall House on the Wild Atlantic Way. It was established in 1215 by the Normans and is located in the well-known fishing village of Baltimore, West Cork.

Throughout the years, the Castle has had many fascinating owners and occupants, including the first Norman settler Sleynie, the local O'Driscoll clan and the famous Fineen the Rover, the Spanish Crown, Cromwellian troops, and many more. Patrick and Bernie McCarthy bought Baltimore Castle in disrepair in 1997 and methodically renovated it over eight years. They have been there since 2005.

For adults, entry to Baltimore Castle is only €5.00. Children are welcome to visit for free!

A walk into the Great Hall on the first level, which has furniture, tapestries, and a history of the Castle dating back 800 years. A pirate display depicting Baltimore's pirate history, including "The Sack of Baltimore" in 1631.

A perspective of archaeological elements on the Castle grounds, as well as an exhibit of archaeological artifacts. A climb up to the battlements affords an unobstructed view of the roof repair as well as a stunning vista of Baltimore Harbor and the islands.

Visit the Cork Public Museum

Cork Public Museum is Ireland's oldest municipal museum, commemorating its 75th anniversary in 2020. The museum is situated in two buildings: a Georgian-style home from the mid-nineteenth century and a contemporary expansion that opened in 2005. The historic museum building was once Charles Beamish's private mansion, a member of the famous brewing family.

You've come to the right place! Admission to the museum is absolutely free, although any gift is greatly appreciated.

The museum houses a superb collection of silver, pottery, and other items related to Cork's civic life. The museum also has a comprehensive portrayal of Cork's archaeology and medieval history. There are also exhibition rooms in three permanent locations. The displays change every three months.

Historic Military Fort in County Cork

Charles Fort is the place to be for those Funstackers interested in learning more about Ireland's military heritage. Built atop the remnants of Blarney Castle, which played an important part during the Siege of Kinsale in 1601. During the Williamite Wars, Charles Fort was involved in some of the most amazing events in Irish history, including a 13-day siege. The star-shaped construction has been meticulously conserved, and there is a wealth of information to be found around every corner.

Admission is Free

Zip Lining and Rope Swings in County Cork

Calling all thrill seekers: it's time to descend into a world of adventure at Zipit in County Cork. Zipit's circuits are built inside a forest and contain zip lines, swinging logs, cargo nets, and rope bridges. All tasks are color-coded and increasingly more difficult, with green being the easiest and orange, white, blue, and red being the most difficult.

Zipit Farran Park

Zipit Farran Park is one of Ireland's largest outdoor high rope adventure parks, located in Farran Forest Park on the southern bank of Inniscarra Lake.

Farran Forest Park features plenty of parking, restrooms, and a playground. A wildlife area and a huge duck pond are further significant features. The wildlife enclosure is home to a small herd of red and fallow deer, which may be seen from the Enclosure Trail, which follows the border fence. A woodland ecology exhibit center has been constructed from an ancient shooting lodge close to the wildlife enclosure. Climbing and zipping activities for adults and children are offered, making this a wonderful day out for the whole family.

Cork City is just 20 minutes away from Zipit Farran Park.

A minimum age of 7 years is required.

Prices range from €15 and €35, depending on the age and number of circuits.

Bookings for groups and schools are available.

There are birthday, business, team development, and school travel packages available.

Visit Nano Nagle Place in Cork

Nano Nagle Place is an unexpected sanctuary in the heart of Cork City, celebrating Nano Nagle's vision of empowerment for a modern world via education, community involvement, and spiritual connection.

The complex includes a museum, history rooms, gardens, the delicious Good Day Deli, a design and gift store, and a Cork-themed book shop in the museum. Several educational organizations are housed in the beautifully restored convent buildings. Come experience Cork at Nano Nagle Place, whether you're a native or a guest.

From Tuesday through Sunday, the museum is open six days a week. It is open from 10:00 a.m. to 5:00 p.m. The museum is unfortunately closed on Mondays.

If Nano Nagle were still living today, she would be the type of person to get the Nobel Prize. Before she died in 1784, Nano had established seven schools for underprivileged children across Cork City, an almshouse for needy women, and, most famously, the Presentation Order, which continues her education and social inclusion work to this day. Honoria Nagle was born in 1718 to a rich Catholic family and was given the nickname Nano by her father. The Nagle family's residence in Ballygriffin, near Mallow, was located on the banks of the Blackwater River.

Wakeboarding in County Cork

Looking for a new and exciting water sport? Wakeboarding is the newest exciting water sport to take over the world, and there are two parks to select from at Ballyhass Wake Park. Both parks will always be operational; during off-peak hours, they may only have one park open with one operator, so you may select which one you want to shred when you arrive.

Other times, you will be required to pick the park while making your reservation. Beginners should try to learn in the west park if feasible, however, we may still teach in both parks. The coaches are available to help you stand for the first time or land your first trick, regardless of your skill level.

Godfather Breakfast Challenge Cork

Forget your usual English breakfast and take on the Godfather Breakfast Challenge, which includes a mouthwatering quantity of scran. 8 Horgan's Irish sausages, 6 smoked rashers, 6oz sirloin steak, 4 hash browns, 4 slices of Clonakilty black and white pudding, 2 fried eggs, 2 scrambled eggs, 2 bowls of chips, 3 fried tomatoes, 1 bowl of baked beans, 1 bowl of sautéed mushrooms, 1 bowl of fried onion rings, All washed down with a bucket of tea or coffee, you have 2.5 hours to eat this breakfast.

What food challenges can I do in Cork?

Take on a monstrous breakfast at Tonys Bistro.

Tonys Bistro is going to make you an impossible offer: if you finish this gut-busting dinner, you'll receive your money back!

The price is €29.95, and

If you finish the challenge, you will be able to eat for free.

Rock Climbing, Hiking, and more in Co. Kerry

If you want to venture outside Kerry, you're in luck because the county has one of the most extensive and tallest mountain ranges in Ireland. It may be frightening to navigate the mountain on your own; nevertheless, Kerry Climbing is here to give you the ideal mountain trip! Kerry Climbing is the best way to begin your trip in Carrauntoohil since they are tailored to your degree of skill, fitness, experience, or goals, as well as the landscape you desire to view.

Outdoor Activities Co. Cork

It's time to add this one to your stack, fun stackers. If you enjoy outdoor sports, you will enjoy the challenges available at Outdoors Ireland in Cork! They provide a variety of exciting outdoor activities such as bushcraft, mountain climbing, and kayaking! Is Cork home to any adventure parks?

Yes! Outdoors Ireland, located directly near Ross Castle and stationed on Lough Leane, offers a variety of demanding outdoor adventures for everyone!

If you're looking for a fun day out for the whole family, head to Outdoors Ireland, which has a variety of activities suitable for any occasion. So, what are you holding out for? Take in some fresh air and have some fun!

There are several activities and bookings to select from.

Activities for participants of all levels of expertise are available from 9:30 a.m. to 5:30 p.m.

Mountain skills training costs £200 per participant.

Training is available for any activity.

CHAPTER EIGHT

CORK Money Saving Tips

Cork is a lovely and dynamic city with something for everyone, although it may be pricey. *Here are a few money-saving suggestions for your vacation to Cork:*

- Purchase a Cork City Pass. This card provides free entrance to several of the city's best attractions as well as unrestricted public transit use.

- Consider staying at a hostel or guesthouse. Hostels and guesthouses are excellent ways to save money on lodging, especially if you're traveling on a tight budget.

- Eat at nearby establishments. Avoid tourist traps and instead dine at local restaurants. You'll get great cuisine for less money.

- Make the most of free activities. There are several free activities in Cork, such as visiting the English Market, strolling around Fitzgerald's Park, or attending a traditional Irish music session.

- Prepare your food. Consider making your own meals if you're living in a hostel or apartment.

This is an excellent method to save money on food, particularly if you're traveling in a group.

- Bring your own food and beverages. This will save you money on overpriced meals and beverages at tourist destinations or airports.
- Make use of public transit. Cork has an excellent public transportation system that is reasonably priced.
- Make use of student discounts. If you are a student, please bring your student ID. Many attractions and companies provide student discounts.
- Request suggestions. If you're not sure where to eat or what to do, seek advice from a local. They'll be delighted to assist you in saving money and having a good time.

CORK Insider Tips

- Explore Cork's pub culture and enjoy live music, cozy atmospheres, and tasty drinks.

- Cork is best explored on foot, so bring comfortable walking shoes.

- Cork is recognized for its farm-to-table eating experiences, so make time to visit the city's many excellent eateries.

- Cork is easily accessible by rail, bus, automobile, and ferry, and there is an international airport about 6.5 kilometers (4 miles) south of the city center.

- Try not to do everything in one trip. Ireland has a lot to offer, so you should be picky about what you want to see and do.

- On the first Wednesday of each month, several heritage sites are free to visit.

- Winter days in Ireland are short, so bear this in mind when planning your visits.

- Approach historic monuments as they were meant to be approached. This entails hiking to them and taking your time to enjoy them.

- Hiking and exploring require the appropriate footwear.

- Know when the buses run and prepare a plan B in case you miss one.

- Get off the beaten track and go exploring. Ireland has many hidden delights to discover.

- Keep in mind the troubled history between Ireland and England.

- Be prepared to encounter a lot of abandoned houses. One of the consequences of Ireland's complicated past is this.

- If you want to visit a private property, you must first obtain permission from the landowner.

- Keep in mind that different sections of Ireland appear extremely different. Some areas are more scenic than others.

- Don't be hesitant to seek assistance from locals. They are typically quite pleasant and willing to assist travelers.

CORK Cultural Tips

Etiquette in Ireland is centered on excellent manners, thus it's not difficult to act correctly when visiting.

1. Handshakes are important.

Handshakes are the most frequent manner to greet people in Ireland. Handshakes are used at both the beginning and finish of a talk. Even if you don't know the individual, using their first name is considered polite in Ireland. A solid handshake with eye contact is expected from all businesses, family members, and friends.

2. Use your inside voice.

Because Americans might be loud at times, it's vital to talk in lower tones. Using loud voices and being disruptive might be considered bad manners in Ireland by some locals.

3. Avoid bringing up politics or religion.

Irish people are not scared to argue or speak their ideas. However, some Irish people are sensitive to religion and prior invasions of their nation. Avoid discussing the IRA and the Troubles, especially in the north. It's just basic etiquette in Ireland to avoid discussing these topics unless the other person brings them up first.

4. Refrain from public displays of affection (PDA).

Hugging, caressing, or being too personal with someone in public is considered impolite in Ireland. In Ireland, avoid using PDAs and respect other people's personal space.

5. Finger twitch while driving is polite.

It is appropriate Irish etiquette to recognize other drivers if you are on a Self-Drive Tour in Ireland and exploring the tiny country roads at modest speeds. Either by raising a hand or even a finger on the driving wheel. Even if you don't know the driver, Irish people welcome others on the road in this manner because it is a courteous thing to do.

6. Pub etiquette in Ireland.

A "rounds" method is employed at a bar with a group of friends. Each participant will offer to purchase a round for everyone in their party and take turns. Those who do not make an offer to buy a round may be deemed impolite.

7. Gift giving.

When visiting Ireland, if you are welcomed to a friend's or relative's house, you should bring a modest gift as a show of your thanks. Flowers, a bottle of Cabernet, or some chocolate Roses are considered excellent travel etiquette in Ireland.

8. Don't smoke in public places.

Since March of 2004, it has been forbidden to smoke in an enclosed public location. Many bars will have dedicated smoking areas. If you smoke, avoid lighting up indoors and be aware of how your cigarette smoke may influence others.

9. Swearing.

Many visitors to Ireland are taken aback by how frequently the Irish use the words "God," "Jesus," or the "F-word" in everyday discourse. It's not considered profanity by many Irish people. If you hear it, simply ignore it and do not answer. It's not meant to startle anyone; it's just a poor habit.

10. Inhaling in agreement.

If they agree with anything expressed, many Irish may take short breaths or inhale. Please do not be concerned and inquire if they have a respiratory problem.

11. Multiple "byes" for ending a conversation on the phone.

If you've ever overheard an Irish person on the phone, you'll note that they say "bye" several times before hanging up. Just roll with it and get into a habit of repeating, "Bye, bye, bye, bye, bye, bye" while closing on the phone!" This is proper manners in Ireland.

12. Phrases not to say

I know you'll be tempted to greet folks with "Top of the Morning," or say "May the Road Rise to Meet You," or even call an Irish person a "Mick" in your best Irish brogue. However, unless it's in a poor movie, Irish people never utter such things. Some could even consider it disrespectful and impolite in Ireland.

CHAPTER NINE

10 Best Day Trips from CORK (By a Local!)

While there are many fantastic tour companies offering day trips from Cork, some of which I'll name below, I honestly feel that hiring a vehicle is the best way to see lovely Cork.

Road journeys are endlessly enjoyable in Ireland, and having your own car allows you to stop whenever you want, visit lovely tiny cafés and restaurants, and linger into the sunset for supper in a local eatery if that tickles your fancy.

There are many amazing spots to see in Ireland; here are a few of the best that can be reached on a day trip from Cork.

1. Clonakilty and Inchydoney Beach

Combining Clonakilty with Inchydoney Beach makes for an excellent day excursion from Cork.

Clonakilty
I must begin with one of my favorite Cork day excursions. Clonakilty is consistently ranked as one of the most beautiful towns in Ireland, as well as one of the cleanest.

The attraction of this vibrant West Cork town resides in the sense of community you get from the moment you walk down the street, as well as the lovely store facades adorned in flower boxes, cute eateries, and pride in "keeping things local."

It's also a famous place for live music, with many of the local pubs and music venues rated as the best in Cork County, frequently attracting big musicians from Ireland and abroad.

There's a lot to do in such a little town. The Model Railway Village, which contains miniature model representations of all the major towns in West Cork and is especially delightful to visit with young children, is a must-see.

A tiny tourist train may also carry visitors throughout the town and as far as the model railway village.

Stop at the vibrant Sticky Bun Cafe for a hearty Irish breakfast and, maybe, some Clonakilty Black Pudding on a toasted sandwich (this town is famous for!). Then, get back in your car and travel to the lovely Inchydoney beach.

Inchydoney Beach

Inchydoney Beach is consistently considered one of the most beautiful beaches in Ireland by the Irish people.

Arriving here on a summer day and seeing the gorgeous waves, the ice cream truck patiently waiting for customers, and people sitting outside the hotel with a nice pint of Bulmers in hand puts a great grin on my face.

Rent surfboards from the beach, which has lifeguards on duty most of the year (look for the flags), or simply spend the afternoon swimming in the frigid Atlantic without a wetsuit.

Take a snooze or go for a long walk on the beach for a more peaceful day at the beach. The Inchydoney Island Hotel provides a lovely background to the bay and is a nice spot for lunch or a drink.

Clonakilty is around a 45-minute drive from Cork City, with an additional 15-minute journey to Inchydoney. If you don't want to drive, GetYourGuide offers a comprehensive West Cork day excursion that includes a stop in Clonakilty.

2. Cobh

This is one of my favorite day trips via rail from Cork. Cork's Kent Station has direct rail service to Cobh. You may also visit one of Cork's greatest castles while you're there.

Check out the Titanic Experience in Cobh, which depicts the tale of the Titanic and how the last people to board the ship did so exactly here in Cobh (then known as Queenstown) before setting sail for the first and last time.

Cobh is also home to the majestic St. Coleman's Cathedral, the "deck of cards" buildings, which make for fascinating images, and where you can board a boat to see the historic Spike Island – however, this may require an additional day trip!

3. Gougane Barra and Glengarriff

Combining Gougane Barra and Glengarriff makes for an excellent day excursion from Cork.

Gougane Bara
Day tour from Cork to Gougane Barra

The modest Gougane Barra Hotel, staring across the lake and the picture-perfect church, is still one of Ireland's most beautiful hidden secrets.

Long walks around the lake and up through the neighboring woodland and hills can be taken before stopping at the hotel for a nice cup of tea and perhaps some cake.

Glengarriff

Then, get back in your car and travel via the twisting roads, past fields of joyful sheep and low-hanging mist to Glengarriff, a west Cork beauty.

You may visit the bamboo park, have a walk in the woods, and even swim in the beautiful blue pool.

This town is quite lovely, with pretty cafés and bars, and is wonderful for souvenir shopping. It is also where you can take boat excursions out to the magnificent Garnish Island, where you may spot wild seals and many rare species along the route.

4. Baltimore and The Islands

Baltimore is a well-kept secret. It's a charming fishing and sailing community in West Cork that serves as a gateway to several of the surrounding islands.

Most of the year, it is calm and tranquil, but in the summer, the population swells with people from all over Cork, Dublin, and Ireland flocking to Baltimore for week-long sailing courses, summer staycations, or to spend time in beautiful summer houses.

I was fortunate enough to spend nearly 15 summers of my childhood down here, learning to swim, row, and sail — and perhaps even learning to drink at one of the many house parties I attended!

Enjoy a leisurely trek up to the beacon for panoramic views of the harbor, or venture out to Sherkin Island, Cape Clear, or Hare Island, all of which have frequent ferries.

On a warm day, the atmosphere is simply incomparable, with live music typically playing outside the Waterfront Bar while people wait for some of Cork's best pizzas and look forward to another amazing West Cork sunset.

Baltimore is roughly an hour and a half drive from Cork City, so if feasible, stay for the night and make it a two-day excursion.

5. Cork's Southern Coastal Route

If you're looking for a scenic drive around Cork, this is one of my favorites. If you have your car, it is by far one of the greatest day trips in Cork.

I don't believe "Cork's Southern Coastal Route" is the official name, but rather one of my favorite drives.

The Wild Atlantic Way is officially believed to finish in Kinsale. This is a little harsh because one of the most gorgeous drives is following the Cork coastline south (or east) to Crosshaven, going through charming fishing villages, coastal towns, and breathtaking cliffs, coves, beaches, and peninsulas.

Begin your journey in Cork and go to Carrigaline, then on to Crosshaven, which is home to the world's oldest Yacht Club and hosts a massive sailing competition every two years known as "Cork Week."I don't believe "Cork's Southern Coastal Route" is the official name, but rather one of my favorite drives.

The Wild Atlantic Way is officially believed to finish in Kinsale. This is a little harsh because one of the most gorgeous drives is following the Cork coastline south (or east) to Crosshaven, going through charming fishing villages, coastal towns, and breathtaking cliffs, coves, beaches, and peninsulas.

Begin your journey in Cork and go to Carrigaline, then on to Crosshaven, which is home to the world's oldest Yacht Club and hosts a massive sailing competition every two years known as "Cork Week."

From here, visit Camden Fort, which overlooks Cork Harbour and Cobh, before continuing to the lovely beaches of Fountainstown and Roberts Cove, where there are some lovely coastal cliff climbs.

Drive on to Oysterhaven, which has a big activity center where youngsters can learn to sail, windsurf, and kayak, as well as a variety of other enjoyable team-building activities.

Finally, drive to Kinsale, stopping at Charles Fort and James Fort along the way, then stopping at the beautiful Old Head of Kinsale and Garretstown Beach for superb coastline views.

6. Blarney Castle and Kinsale

You can't visit Cork without seeing Blarney Castle, one of the city's most recognized attractions if not one of the most famous sites to see in all of Ireland.

Blarney Castle

Blarney Castle is located about 15 minutes outside of Cork's city center and does not require a whole day to explore, therefore it is best to combine with a visit to a town outside of the city, such as Kinsale or even Cobh.

You may take a bus from the city to Blarney, join an organized tour, or drive yourself, then pay the admission charge to visit the castle and grounds and, of course, kiss the famed Blarney Stone!

If you choose to go to Kinsale, you may drive or take a bus back to the city, then another bus from the station down to Kinsale.

Kinsale Town

Kinsale is a popular gourmet destination in Ireland, with several excellent pubs, cafés, and seafood restaurants, as well as typical fish and chip shops.

Kinsale has enough to offer. It's ideal for souvenir shopping, with plenty of gorgeous art galleries, boutiques, and adorable bookstores to keep you busy for a few hours.

7. Dingle Peninsula

The gorgeous Dingle Peninsula is one of Ireland's most beautiful regions and a must-see on any Ireland road trip. While the travel from Cork is lengthy, it is a very achievable day trip from Cork if you get up early.

Dingle Peninsula
There are also several excellent scheduled bus trips available to make the day's journey less hectic. Even better, you can always stay the night; Dingle has some extremely unusual places to stay!

Dingle, famous for its friendly dolphins, colorful shop fronts, and bustling bar scene, is one of Ireland's most popular tourist destinations, with visitors from all over the world coming here, especially during the summer.

The trip along the Dingle Peninsula from Dingle town, stopping at secluded beaches and stunning cliffs, is unforgettable, especially on a clear day when you can see as far as the Blasket Islands.

Consider sweeping green fields full of fluffy sheep, calm, meandering country roads with grass in the center, friendly residents, long white sandy beaches, and amazing waves for surfing.

If you don't have your car, this highly-rated trip from Cork takes in several of the Dingle Peninsula's main attractions. It's an excellent alternative if you don't feel comfortable driving here.

8. Midleton Distillery and Youghal

One of the simplest day trips from Cork is to the Midleton Jameson Distillery, followed by a visit to Youghal and a lengthy walk on the Eastern beaches.

Jameson Whiskey Distillery

The Jameson Distillery is a great site to stop for a tour behind the scenes of the historic brewery as well as some whiskey sampling. Midleton is usually lovely and worth spending an hour strolling about.

Youghal
Youghal is one of the most well-known coastal towns in County Cork, with visitors from all over the nation flocking here during the summer months to relax on the beach, go swimming, or visit the funfair, or "the merrier."

9. Lakes of Killarney

One of the most popular day excursions in Cork is undoubtedly a visit to the well-known Lakes of Killarney. One of Ireland's most popular and frequented tourist villages is a little over an hour's drive from Cork City.

Killarney

Traditional horse and jaunting carts drive cheerful tourists down the streets towards Muckross Park and Gardens, while pubs line the streets, all with live traditional music day and night.

You may take a boat across the lakes or spend the day roaming among the gardens, lakes, and up to spectacular waterfalls such as the Torc Waterfall.

While incredibly touristic, Killarney is a lovely and colorful town that is well worth a visit. The surrounding terrain is spectacular, and there are several fantastic drives around the Ring of Kerry that depart from here.

10. Cliffs of Moher

The Cliffs of Moher are one of Ireland's most popular (if not the most popular) tourist attractions. A visit here is essential.

Cliffs Of Moher

The travel from Cork to the Cliffs of Moher takes around 2.5 hours, but it's entirely possible in a day. Of course, you could drive there, but there's a fantastic day excursion available for about $50. It's a fantastic deal!

Starting in Cork, you'll travel to Limerick, stopping on the banks of the Shannon. From there, you'll go to the Cliffs of Moher, where you'll get 90 minutes to see the natural beauty.

After that, take a scenic drive down the Atlantic coast, then visit the Burren Region and the Bunratty Castle.

CHAPTER TEN

3 DAYS IN CORK: The Perfect CORK Itinerary for First-Time Visitors

Whether you consider yourself a leisurely traveler or simply want to make a quick tour of Cork, the city has plenty to offer that you will never forget. Cork's charm will keep you firmly in its grasp, making you wish you could remain forever.

If you just have one day in Cork, bring your walking shoes. The city center is not vast, but it is attractive, therefore you should explore it on foot. You'll have time to browse at the English Market, listen to buskers, visit a museum, and sip a glass of Murphy's.

Locals in Cork enjoy a well-tapped glass of locally made Murphy's stout with its easily creamy finish.

If you can prolong your stay in Cork to two days, you may also enjoy the riches of the surrounding counties. Cobh should be at the top of your agenda, and no trip to Cork is complete without you seeing the famed Deck of Cards Houses.

The ultimate prize is three days in Cork, which will allow you to explore the city at your leisure, take a day trip or two, and enjoy an evening out on the town.

Cork is easy to reach because of its well-connected transportation hubs. Cork Airport, which serves both local and international flights, serves the city. Visitors may take a bus or cab from the airport to the city center, which is only a 15-minute drive away.

If you're traveling from Dublin, the trip from Dublin to Cork takes around 3 hours, although there are lots of places to stop along the route. You may compare automobile rental costs in Ireland by visiting Rentalcars.com.

Cork Kent Station is the principal railway station, having direct links to Dublin, Limerick, and other important Irish towns for people who want to travel by train.

The station is centrally positioned, making it simple to navigate and reach your destination.

Getting about Cork is simple once you've arrived. The downtown area is compact and accessible, with most attractions and facilities within easy reach. There are buses and taxis available for longer distances, as well as bike rentals for those who prefer to explore on two wheels.

Cork is also well-connected to neighboring cities, giving it an excellent base for exploring the surrounding area. Day tours to the must-see Blarney Castle or any of the picturesque communities surrounding the city are available.

Cork is a simple travel to and from, with a range of transportation options and an easy-to-navigate city center. Cork will delight and inspire you whether you are a seasoned traveler or a first-time visitor.

DAY ONE
Cork's City Centre

Spend one day in Cork getting to know the city and discovering all the greatest sites. If you want to spend a portion of your day sightseeing with a guide, this historical walking tour is for you.

The English Market

Start your day with a trip around the English Market, a Corkian experience. As you start your day, browse the freshly baked goodies, smell the brewing coffee, and get a bite to eat.

This market has been open since 1788 and still provides personal over-the-counter service, giving the entire market a warm and welcoming feel.

Get to know the people and feel the legendary Cork spirit by chatting with a sausage salesperson or a baker before 9 a.m. You may also book a cuisine tour for later in the day here.

Shandon Mile

Cork City Council has created a delightful 1-mile walk around the city's most historic areas, complete with a guide documenting all of the key history that went through the streets.

The walk begins in Daunt's Square, immediately outside the English Market, and follows a nearly round circuit. Along the mile, there are ten information panels to keep you informed and on the proper track.

St. Anne's Church, the Butter Museum, and the Shandon Bridge across the River Lee are among the significant landmarks along the mile. Inside St. Anne's Church, pretend to be Quasimodo for a while as you ring the famed Cork bells and climb the 132 steps to the top of the tower for a spectacular 360-degree panorama of the city.

Cork City Gaol

Ireland's gaols (or prisons if you don't understand Gaelic) are a distinctive element of the country's history. Architecturally, it is a spectacular structure, but Cork Gaol tours also provide a fascinating insight into the country's civil war past, which still resonates in the contemporary context.

Cork is susceptible to mild afternoon rains, so try to time your visit to avoid the precipitation.

Explore Cork's Historic Sites

Cork's environment is responsible for much of its allure. The city is tiny and notably less touristy than Dublin, allowing you to explore genuine Ireland.

Walking along the river or exploring picturesque streets may easily occupy a day in Cork, but there are a few more historical places to see.

If you wish to go back in time, visit Elizabeth Fort, Blackrock Castle, Saint Fin Barre's Cathedral, and Cork Public Museum.

Mutton Lane Inn

If you just go to one bar in Cork (which would be a disservice to yourself), make it this one. It is one of Cork's oldest bars, yet its charm pervades every whiskey-soaked nook.

It's directly close to the English Market, nestled away in a narrow path where sheep used to be herded into the market. It now only guides lambs to the watering hole.

DAY TWO

Cobh, Midleton, Kinsale, or Whale Watching

If you have two days in Cork, you may spend one day touring the city and the other seeing the surrounding towns.

There is public transportation to most of them, as well as different guided excursions or shuttles, such as this full-day trip or this day tour, but if you are short on time, renting a vehicle is the most effective option. These are some of the most beautiful towns in the Cork area.

Cobh

If there is just one hamlet to see in Cork, it is Cobh. Spike Island, the Titanic Experience, and the picture-perfect church with the vividly colored stacked buildings in the foreground are only 30 minutes away in town.

You could easily spend a whole day in Cobh, but try to start with breakfast at one of the numerous beautiful bistros, then head to at least one more town in County Cork. Cobh is the final station on the Dublin-Cork route.

Midleton

Midleton is a traditional Irish town well known for housing the Jameson Distillery. Take a distillery tour to understand how this golden elixir is manufactured and to sample its varied flavors.

The two villages are only 20 minutes apart, so this may be a pleasant second stop following a visit to Cobh. If the weather is pleasant, you might wish to visit one of the neighboring Blue Flag beaches or the bustling farmers market.

Kinsale

This hidden gem is the most southern town on the Wild Atlantic Way, and it is vibrant beyond belief. It is also one of Ireland's greatest culinary treasures, with a Michelin-starred restaurant and two more recommended by the highly regarded guide.

With just two days in Cork, golf may not be your priority, but if you have an uncontrollable need to tee off, head to

Old Head Golf Links. At one of the most unusual courses in the world, you will play among ancient ruins on the brink of some very stunning cliffs.

Whale Watching in County Cork

West Cork is the ideal spot to charter a whale-watching excursion, and there are various places from which to embark. Courtmacsherry is the nearest to Cork City, about an hour away. Baltimore, Ireland's most popular whale-watching town, is located further west along the coast.

Minke and humpback whales are the most regularly seen, however, killer whales and fin whales have also been observed. There are excursions available all year (weather permitting), and various species can be seen at different periods of the year.

Tours typically run 2-2.5 hours, so you can easily do this in the morning or afternoon and still have time to visit other attractions in Cork.

DAY THREE

Blarney Castle or County Cork Hiking

Those who have more than 48 hours in Cork might spend their final day doing more time-consuming activities.

Blarney Castle

Blarney Castle is one of the most popular tourist attractions in Cork, if not the entire Republic. It is fewer than 10 kilometers from Cork City, yet it takes many hours to truly appreciate the castle.

Everyone is rushing to kiss the famous Blarney Stone at the top of the castle to obtain the gift of the gab. The castle, on the other hand, has a lot more to offer. It should be mentioned that kissing the blarney stone appears to be easier than it is, and those who are afraid of heights should reconsider.

Dangling upside down over a cliff becomes very real very quickly, and you don't want to risk a freakout in front of a crowd of curious bystanders. Despite the 128 tiny steps to the summit, the vista across the rolling green meadows is spectacular.

The castle grounds include around 60 acres, and it is worthwhile to wander around and enjoy the peace and quiet. Enter the toxic garden at your peril, see the dungeon and witch's kitchen, take a stroll through the lush lanes and garden paths, and marvel at the bizarre flora in the carnivorous garden and fern forest.

Go Hiking

The cliffs on Ireland's outskirts are, in a word, magnificent. Cork has some breathtaking coastline scenery, and the Wild Atlantic Way begins on this side of the nation.

If you have time, you should consider doing one of the short coastal walks, particularly the Ballycotton Cliff Walk. The walk is 3.5 kilometers each way (7 kilometers overall — it is not a round path) and is appropriate for persons of all fitness levels.

Another popular one is the Old Head of Kinsale Loop, which is just 6 kilometers long and passes through the old Celtic Fort and the black and white lighthouse. Another beautiful walk is the Lough Hyne Hill Walk, where you can saunter down to the lough and swim or kayak if the weather is right.

If you don't want to climb, you may view portions of the Wild Atlantic Way by visiting the Ring of Kerry. You may drive yourself or join a tour here.

Ballycotton Cliff Walk-Catch a Sunset

A spectacular sunset is one of the nicest ways to finish any vacation. There are various locations in and around the city where you may do so.

The hills at Frankfield, Rober's Cove, and Sheep's Head are all breathtaking locations where you may conclude your day in style.

Conclusion

Finally, we encourage you to go on an exciting journey to the heart of Cork, Ireland. We hope that after exploring every nook and corner of this interesting city, from its historic past to its dynamic present, you've been inspired to plan your journey.

Cork, with its rich history, magnificent surroundings, and friendly population, provides something for every tourist. Cork welcomes you with open arms, whether you're a history buff looking to unearth the city's secrets, a gourmet seeking gastronomic pleasures, or a nature lover looking to explore the gorgeous coastline.

With our thorough guide, you'll be well-prepared for your Cork adventure, equipped with insider insights, crucial information, and must-see suggestions. Cork offers a voyage packed with discovery and enjoyment, from the busy English Market to the calm beaches, ancient sites to hidden secrets.

As you sample the local food, raise a glass in one of Cork's lovely pubs, and immerse yourself in the city's cultural tapestry, you'll discover that Cork is more than a destination; it's an experience that will stay with you long after you've gone home.

We hope this guide has sparked your wanderlust and given you the skills to make your Cork vacation a reality. Whether you're a first-time tourist or a seasoned traveler, Cork has unlimited options and experiences waiting to be made.

So pack your luggage, prepare your senses, and prepare to discover the charm of Cork. We look forward to welcoming you to this fascinating city, where history, culture, and natural beauty combine to provide an experience unlike any other.

Your Cork adventure awaits—see you soon in Rebel County!

NOMAD NICK

Printed in Great Britain
by Amazon